||||| || ||||||| || |||| || || |||
I0117203

Stoicism: Knowledge, Reason, Harmony

ISBN: 978-0-244-17373-9

Andreas Sofroniou, 2019 © Copyright

Andreas Sofroniou, 2019 © Copyright

Stoicism: Knowledge, Reason, Harmony

ISBN: 978-0-244-17373-9

Contents   *Page*

Andreas Sofroniou

Stoicism: Virtue, Reality, Politics

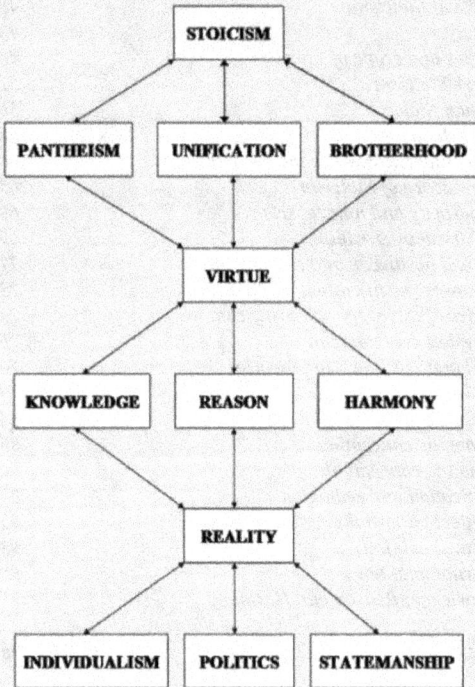

```
                    ┌──────────────┐
                    │   STOICISM   │
                    └──────────────┘

┌──────────────┐   ┌──────────────┐   ┌──────────────┐
│  PANTHEISM   │   │ UNIFICATION  │   │ BROTHERHOOD  │
└──────────────┘   └──────────────┘   └──────────────┘

                    ┌──────────────┐
                    │    VIRTUE    │
                    └──────────────┘

┌──────────────┐   ┌──────────────┐   ┌──────────────┐
│  KNOWLEDGE   │   │    REASON    │   │   HARMONY    │
└──────────────┘   └──────────────┘   └──────────────┘

                    ┌──────────────┐
                    │   REALITY    │
                    └──────────────┘

┌──────────────┐   ┌──────────────┐   ┌──────────────┐
│INDIVIDUALISM │   │   POLITICS   │   │ STATEMANSHIP │
└──────────────┘   └──────────────┘   └──────────────┘
```

Andreas Sofroniou

Stoicism

Stoic: meaning and origin

Stoic is the term used for a member of a philosophical school founded by Zeno of Citium *c.*300 BC.

The name derives from the fact that he taught in the *Stoa poikile* ('Painted Colonnade') at Athens. Zeno's followers propounded various metaphysical systems, united chiefly by their ethical implications.

All were variants on the pantheistic theme that the world constitutes a single, organically unified and benevolent whole, in which apparent evil results only from our limited view.

Their philosophy had at its core the beliefs that virtue is based on:

- Knowledge;

- Reason is the governing principle of nature;

- Individuals should live in harmony with nature.

The vicissitudes of life were viewed with equanimity: pleasure, pain, and even death were irrelevant to true happiness.

In time, the idea that only the consummately wise man (the philosopher) could attain virtue was challenged, and Stoicism became more relevant to the reality of politics and statesmen.

This, the Stoic belief in the brotherhood of man, helped the philosophy to make a real impact in later republican Rome, upon such men as the young Cato (whose suicide brought him a martyr's fame), Brutus, and Cicero.

Later it underlay much aristocratic opposition to the emperors, but even so its disciples included Seneca, tutor and adviser to Nero and the emperor Marcus Aurelius.

Pantheism

Pantheism is the doctrine that the universe conceived of as a whole is God and, conversely, that there is no God but the combined substance, forces, and laws that are manifested in the existing universe. The cognate doctrine of panentheism asserts that God includes the universe as a part though not the whole of his being.

Both "pantheism" and "panentheism" are terms of recent origin, coined to describe certain views of the relationship between God and the world that are different from that of traditional theism. As reflected in the prefix "pan-" (Greek *pas*, "all"), both of the terms stress the all-embracing inclusiveness of God, as compared with his separateness as emphasized in many versions of theism.

On the other hand, pantheism and panentheism, since they stress the theme of immanence—i.e., of the indwelling presence of God—are themselves versions of theism conceived in its broadest meaning. Pantheism stresses the identity between God and the world, panentheism (Greek *en*, "in") that the world is included in God but that God is more than the world.

6

The adjective "pantheist" was introduced by the Irish Deist John Toland in the book *Socinianism Truly Stated* (1705). The noun "pantheism" was first used in 1709 by one of Toland's opponents. The term "panentheism" appeared much later, in 1828.

Although the terms are recent, they have been applied retrospectively to alternative views of the divine being as found in the entire philosophical traditions of both East and West.

Free will

Free will refers to the philosophical problem of understanding how it is possible for people to be held morally responsible for their actions, given that there is reason for thinking that what they do is determined by causes.

The problem of free will originates in the context of theology: if God is omniscient and omnipotent, it appears to follow that everything people do is foreknown by God, and determined by God's will.

The same problem, in a secular context, is often seen in terms of a clash between morality and science: whereas moral practices (such as punishment) require our actions to be free, science tells us that everything we do is governed by the inexorable laws of nature; the deterministic view is of the world, including people, as just a vast machine, all of whose movements could in principle, given enough information, be predicted by physical science.

Two important views of the nature of free will are those of the libertarian and the compatibilist.

Libertarians, such as Kant, hold that free will consists in the ability to do otherwise than one in fact does, that is, power of choice, and that this involves a suspension of the laws of nature. Libertarians have difficulty in explaining how this is possible, and Kant thought that for there to be free will, people had to be thought of as being in some sense outside the bounds of nature.

Compatibilists such as Hume, by contrast, deny that this much is needed for free will. They hold instead that a person acts freely so long as he is not constrained by external forces, such as the will of another person. For a compatibilist it is enough for a person to have acted freely that he knew what he was doing and that his action expressed his desires or character.

Compatibilists face in turn the problem of explaining why the factors which determine a person's desires or character, such as their genetic make-up or upbringing, over which they have no control, should not be regarded as depriving them of free will.

In humans, the power or capacity to choose among alternatives or to act in certain situations independently of natural, social, or divine restraints. Free will is denied by some proponents of determinism.

Arguments for free will are based on the subjective experience of freedom, on sentiments of guilt, on revealed religion, and on the universal supposition of responsibility for personal actions that underlies the concepts of law, reward, punishment, and incentive.

In theology the existence of free will must be reconciled with God's omniscience and goodness (in allowing people to choose badly) and with divine grace, which allegedly is necessary for any meritorious act.

8

A prominent feature of existentialism is the concept of a radical, perpetual, and frequently agonizing freedom of choice. Jean-Paul Sartre (1905–80), for example, spoke of the individual "condemned to be free."

Freedom

Freedom is the condition in which people, individually or collectively, can control their own lives without interference either by other people or by some outside political authority.

In the modern world, the demand for political freedom takes two main forms: the demand of nations that they should throw off foreign rule, and govern themselves through their own political institutions; and the demand of individuals that the state should not interfere in areas of life that are deemed to be private.

This last demand includes specific freedoms such as freedom of expression and worship, freedom of association, and (more controversially) economic freedom in the sense of the freedom to buy, sell, and contract with any willing party.

Political philosophers such as Isaiah Berlin ('Two Concepts of Liberty', 1958) have drawn a distinction between negative and positive senses of freedom, where being negatively free means simply not being prevented or deterred by other people from achieving one's goals, whereas being positively free means having the capacity (the resources, the mental determination, and so on) to achieve those goals.

Freedom, although an important political value, must be limited for its own sake and for the sake of other ends. The best-known principle for deciding this is enunciated in Mill's

9

essay *On Liberty* (1859): people should be free to act as they
like except when their actions cause harm to other people.

Providence

The English word *providence* is derived from the Latin term
providentia, which primarily means foresight or
foreknowledge but also forethought and providence in the
religious sense; thus, Cicero used the phrase the "providence
of the gods" (*deorum providentia*).

The Stoic philosophers thoroughly discussed the significance
of the term *providence*, and some of them wrote treatises on
the subject. A hymn to Zeus written about 300 BCE by
Cleanthes, a Greek poet and philosopher, is a glorification of
the god as a benevolent and foreseeing ruler of the world
and of humankind.

According to Cleanthes, God has planned the world in
accordance with this providence:

- For thee this whole vast cosmos, wheeling round

- The earth, obeys, and where thou leadest

- It follows, ruled willingly by thee.

The author asserts that "naught upon Earth is wrought in
thy despite, O God" and that in Zeus all things are
harmonized. Seneca, a Roman Stoic philosopher, formulates
the belief in providence in one of his dialogues as follows:
humans should believe "that providence rules the world and
that God cares for us."

The Stoic school disagreed with those who believed that the
world was ruled by blind fate; they did not deny that a

10

controlling power exists, but, as everything happens according to a benevolent divine plan, they preferred to call this power providence.

According to the Stoic emperor Marcus Aurelius, God wills everything that happens to human beings, and for that reason nothing that occurs can be considered evil. Stoic ideas about providence influenced Christianity.

In later Latin, after the emperor Augustus (died 14 CE), the word *providence* was used as a designation of the deity. Seneca, for example, wrote that it is proper to apply the term *providence* to God.

Finally, providence was personified as a proper goddess in her own right by Macrobius, a Neoplatonic Roman author, who wrote in defence of paganism about 400 CE.

Truth

Truth is the term used in metaphysics and the philosophy of language, the property of sentences, assertions, beliefs, thoughts, or propositions that are said, in ordinary discourse, to agree with the facts or to state what the case is.

Truth is the aim of belief; falsity is a fault. People need the truth about the world in order to thrive. Truth is important.

Believing what is not true is apt to spoil a person's plans and may even cost him his life. Telling what is not true may result in legal and social penalties.

Conversely, a dedicated pursuit of truth characterizes the good scientist, the good historian, and the good detective. So what is truth, that it should have such gravity and such a central place in people's lives?

11

Correspondence theory

The classic suggestion comes from Aristotle (384–322 BCE): "To say of what is that it is, or of what is not that it is not, is true." In other words, the world provides "what is" or "what is not," and the true saying or thought corresponds to the fact so provided.

This idea appeals to common sense and is the germ of what is called the correspondence theory of truth.

As it stands, however, it is little more than a platitude and far less than a theory. Indeed, it may amount to merely a wordy paraphrase, whereby, instead of saying "that's true" of some assertion, one says "that corresponds with the facts." Only if the notions of fact and correspondence can be further developed will it be possible to understand truth in these terms.

Unfortunately, many philosophers doubt whether an acceptable explanation of facts and correspondence can be given. Facts, as they point out, are strange entities. It is tempting to think of them as structures or arrangements of things in the world.

However, as the Austrian-born philosopher Ludwig Wittgenstein observed, structures have spatial locations, but facts do not. The Eiffel Tower can be moved from Paris to Rome, but the fact that the Eiffel Tower is in Paris cannot be moved anywhere.

Furthermore, critics urge, the very idea of what the facts are in a given case is nothing apart from people's sincere beliefs about the case, which means those beliefs that people take to be true.

Thus, there is no enterprise of first forming a belief or theory about some matter and then in some new process stepping outside the belief or theory to assess whether it corresponds with the facts.

There are, indeed, processes of checking and verifying beliefs, but they work by bringing up further beliefs and perceptions and assessing the original in light of those. In actual investigations, what tells people what to believe is not the world or the facts but how they interpret the world or select and conceptualize the facts.

Coherence and pragmatist theories

Starting in the mid-19th century, this line of criticism led some philosophers to think that they should concentrate on larger theories, rather than sentences or assertions taken one at a time.

Truth, on this view, must be a feature of the overall body of belief considered as a system of logically interrelated components—what is called the "web of belief."

It might be, for example, an entire physical theory that earns its keep by making predictions or enabling people to control things or by simplifying and unifying otherwise disconnected phenomena.

An individual belief in such a system is true if it sufficiently coheres with, or makes rational sense within, enough other beliefs; alternatively, a belief system is true if it is sufficiently internally coherent.

Such were the views of the British idealists, including F.H. Bradley and H.H. Joachim, who, like all idealists, rejected

13

the existence of mind-independent facts against which the truth of beliefs could be determined.

Yet coherentism too seems inadequate, since it suggests that human beings are trapped in the sealed compartment of their own beliefs, unable to know anything of the world beyond.

Moreover, as the English philosopher and logician Bertrand Russell pointed out, nothing seems to prevent there being many equally coherent but incompatible belief systems. Yet at best only one of them can be true.

Some theorists have suggested that belief systems can be compared in pragmatic or utilitarian terms. According to this idea, even if many different systems can be internally coherent, it is likely that some will be much more useful than others.

Thus, one can expect that, in a process akin to Darwinian natural selection, the more useful systems will survive while the others gradually go extinct. The replacement of Newtonian mechanics by relativity theory is an example of this process.

It was in this spirit that the 19th-century American pragmatist philosopher Charles Sanders Peirce said: The opinion which is fated to be ultimately agreed to by all who investigate, is what we mean by the truth, and the object represented in this opinion is the real.

In effect, Peirce's view places primary importance on scientific curiosity, experimentation, and theorizing and identifies truth as the imagined ideal limit of their ongoing progress.

Although this approach may seem appealingly hard-headed, it has prompted worries about how a society, or humanity as a whole, could know at a given moment whether it is following the path toward such an ideal. In practice it has opened the door to varying degrees of scepticism about the notion of truth.

In the late 20th century philosophers such as Richard Rorty advocated retiring the notion of truth in favour of a more open-minded and open-ended process of indefinite adjustment of beliefs. Such a process, it was felt, would have its own utility, even though it lacked any final or absolute endpoint.

Truth conditions

The rise of formal logic (the abstract study of assertions and deductive arguments) and the growth of interest in formal systems (formal or mathematical languages) among many Anglo-American philosophers in the early 20th century led to new attempts to define truth in logically or scientifically acceptable terms.

It also led to a renewed respect for the ancient liar paradox (attributed to the ancient Greek philosopher Epimenides), in which a sentence says of itself that it is false, thereby apparently being true if it is false and false if it is true.

Logicians set themselves the task of developing systems of mathematical reasoning that would be free of the kinds of self-reference that give rise to paradoxes such as that of the liar.

However, this proved difficult to do without at the same time making some legitimate proof procedures impossible. There is good self-reference ("All sentences, including this, are of finite length") and bad self-reference ("This sentence is

15

false") but no generally agreed-upon principle for distinguishing them.

These efforts culminated in the work of the Polish-born logician Alfred Tarski, who in the 1930s showed how to construct a definition of truth for a formal or mathematical language by means of a theory that would assign truth conditions (the conditions in which a given sentence is true) to each sentence in the language without making use of any semantic terms, notably including *truth,* in that language.

While the technical aspects of Tarski's work were much admired and have been much discussed, its philosophical significance remained unclear, in part because T-sentences struck many theorists as less than illuminating. But the weight of philosophical opinion gradually shifted, and eventually this platitudinous appearance was regarded as a virtue and indeed as indicative of the whole truth about truth.

The idea was that, instead of staring at the abstract question "What is truth?," philosophers should content themselves with the particular question "What does the truth of S amount to?"; and for any well-specified sentence, a humble T-sentence will provide the answer.

Deflationism

Philosophers before Tarski, including Gottlob Frege and Frank Ramsey, had suspected that the key to understanding truth lay in the odd fact that putting "It is true that…" in front of an assertion changes almost nothing. It is true that snow is white if and only if snow is white. At most there might be an added emphasis, but no change of topic.

The theory that built on this insight is known as "deflationism" or "minimalism" (an older term is "the redundancy theory").

- Yet, if truth is essentially redundant, why should talk of truth be so common?

- What purpose does the truth predicate serve?

The answer, according to most deflationists, is that *true* is a highly useful device for making generalisations over large numbers of sayings or assertions.

Despite their contention that the truth predicate is essentially redundant, deflationists can allow that truth is important and that it should be the aim of rational inquiry. Indeed, the paraphrases into which the deflationary view renders such claims help to explain why this is so.

While deflationism has been an influential view since the 1970s, it has not escaped criticism. One objection is that it takes the meanings of sentences too much for granted. According to many theorists, including the American philosopher Donald Davidson, the meaning of a sentence is equivalent to its truth conditions.

If deflationism is correct, however, then this approach to sentence meaning might have to be abandoned (because no statement of the truth conditions of a sentence could be any more informative than the sentence itself).

But this in turn is contestable, since deflationists can reply that the best model of what it is to "give the truth conditions" of a sentence is simply that of Tarski, and Tarski uses nothing beyond the deflationists' own notion of truth. If this is right, then saying what a sentence means by giving its truth conditions comes to nothing more than saying what a sentence means.

As indicated above, the realm of truth bearers has been populated in different ways in different theories.

In some it consists of sentences, in others sayings, assertions, beliefs, or propositions. Although assertions and related speech acts are featured in many theories, much work remains to be done on the nature of assertion in different areas of discourse.

Dialectic

Originally, dialectics was a form of logical argumentation but now a philosophical concept of evolution applied to diverse fields including thought, nature, and history.

Among the classical Greek thinkers, the meanings of dialectic ranged from a technique of refutation in debate, through a method for systematic evaluation of definitions, to the investigation and classification of the relationships between specific and general concepts. From the time of the Stoic philosophers until the end of the European Middle Ages, dialectic was more or less closely identified with the discipline of formal logic.

More recently, Immanuel Kant denoted by "transcendental dialectic" the endeavour of exposing the illusion involved in attempting to use the categories and principles of the understanding beyond the bounds of phenomena and possible experience.

G.W.F. Hegel identified dialectic as the tendency of a notion to pass over into its own negation as the result of conflict between its inherent contradictory aspects. Karl Marx and Friedrich Engels adopted Hegel's definition and applied it to social and economic processes.

Virtue and ethics

Virtue

Virtue is the approach to ethics that takes the notion of desirable quality (often conceived as excellence) as fundamental.

Virtue ethics is primarily concerned with traits of character that are essential to human flourishing, not with the enumeration of duties.

It falls somewhat outside the traditional dichotomy between deontological ethics and consequentialism: It agrees with consequentialism that the criterion of an action's being morally right or wrong lies in its relation to an end that has intrinsic value, but more closely resembles deontological ethics in its view that morally right actions are constitutive of the end itself and not mere instrumental means to the end.

Ethics

Ethics is the philosophical study of the nature and grounds of moral thought and action. Ethical theories in this pure sense are sharply distinguished from moral systems, which are directed towards drawing up particular sets of rules by which to live (such as Christian morality), and from practical or applied ethics, the analysis of arguments advanced for particular moral conclusions (such as the rightness or wrongness of abortion).

The most fundamental question in ethics is usually taken to be the justification of morality that is whether or not it can be demonstrated that moral action is rational. Schools of ethics can be divided, very roughly, into three sorts:

- The first, which derives from Aristotle's *Ethics*, gives pride of place to the virtues, such as justice, charity, and generosity, which are thought of as dispositions to act in ways that both tend to the fulfilment of the person who has them and to benefit the society of which he or she is a member.

  Aristotle's ethics are also often described as naturalistic, in that he seeks to exhibit a harmony between morality and human nature.

- The second, which is defended in most depth by Kant, is the school which makes the concept of duty central to morality (called 'deontology'). Kant argued that the only thing which is good in itself (as opposed to merely good as a means) is a 'good will', one which is freely in accordance with duty.

  Knowledge of one's duty, for Kant, follows from a realization that one is a rational being, and thus bound to obey what he called the 'categorical imperative', the requirement to respect all rational beings as autonomous 'ends in themselves'. Kant's views of morality are intimately connected with his view of free will.

- The third school of ethics is utilitarianism whose goal is the 'greatest happiness of the greatest number'.

  Ethical theories may also be divided in another way, according to whether or not they allow that there is such a thing as objective moral truth; Hume, as a

20

subjectivist, held that morality is profoundly rooted in our 'sentiments'.

Ethics in this century has been largely preoccupied with analysing the meaning of moral language, as in Ayer's theory of emotivism, whereby the meaning of a moral statement consists in its expressing an emotional attitude.

Eudaemonism

Eudaemonism in ethics is a self-realisation theory that makes happiness or personal well-being the chief good for man.

The Greek word *eudaimonia* means literally "the state of having a good indwelling spirit, a good genius"; and "happiness" is not at all an adequate translation of this word. Happiness, indeed, is usually thought of as a state of mind that results from or accompanies some actions.

But Aristotle's answers to the question:

"What is *eudaimonia?*"

Namely, that which is "activity in accordance with virtue", or

That which is "contemplation", shows that for him *eudaimonia* was not a state of mind consequent on, or

Accompanying certain activities but is a name for these activities themselves.

"What is *eudaimonia?*" is then the same question as

"What are the best activities of which man is capable?"

21

Later moralists, however—for instance, the 18th- and 19th-century British utilitarians Jeremy Bentham and John Stuart Mill—defined happiness as pleasure and the absence of pain.

Others, still regarding happiness as a state of mind, have tried to distinguish it from pleasure on the grounds that it is mental, not bodily; enduring, not transitory; and rational, not emotional. But these distinctions are open to question.

A temporal dimension was added to eudaemonism in ancient times by Solon, who said, "Call no man happy till he is dead," suggesting that happiness and its opposite pertain, in their broadest sense, to the full course of one's life. Contemporary moralists have tended to avoid the term.

Reason

Reason (rationality) is the faculty of making judgements and inferences. Reason may be divided into theoretical and practical reason. Theoretical reason aims at true belief; practical reason aims at right action.

The operations of reason can also be divided into deductive and inductive forms, and can to some extent be formally described by logic. Reason is distinguished from other faculties, such as perception, emotion, and imagination.

The relative power of reason and desire is a central philosophical question; Hume famously claimed that practical reason can only ever be the 'slave of the passions'.

Possession of reason is often said to provide the essential difference between man and other members of the animal kingdom.

Descartes described human reason as 'universal', meaning that a being that has reason is not limited to a fixed stock of responses, and connected the faculty of reason with the ability to use language.

The existence of reason provides a major challenge for a naturalistic view of persons.

Naturalism

Naturalism (in philosophy), an outlook which stresses the role of facts about human nature in explaining human thought, and, more generally, sees human beings firmly as parts of the natural order.

Naturalism is broadly opposed to religious and metaphysical outlooks. Thus naturalism is frequently (although not necessarily) associated with materialism and a high estimation of the physical sciences.

Naturalist theories have both an explanatory and a justificatory aspect. They seek in the first instance to show that it is possible to explain why we think the way we do in terms of facts about our natural constitution; and they then seek to show that by appealing to those facts it is possible to provide as much of a justification for our ways of thinking as can reasonably be demanded.

There are important strains of naturalism in the philosophies of Hume and Wittgenstein. Ethical naturalism regards moral judgements as grounded in, and perhaps even as deducible from, facts about human nature.

Existentialism

Existentialism refers to a movement in mid-20th-century continental philosophy. In the post-war years it gripped the imagination of many thinkers, writers, and artists. Its appeal lay partly in its ability to reflect the alienation and experience of atrocity in 20th-century Europe.

Existentialist philosophers speculated about the nature of reality, but subordinated traditional metaphysical and epistemological questions to an anthropocentric perspective, in which there takes place a dramatic, often tragic, confrontation between man and the world.

Existentialist thought tends to disparage scientific knowledge, particularly psychology, in so far as it claims to be a science, and to insist on the absence of objective values, stressing instead the reality and significance of human freedom.

Influenced by Kierkegaard, existentialism gave rise to a tradition of Christian existentialism, but the best-known exponents of existentialism in its atheistic form are Heidegger and Sartre.

Existentialism cannot be easily identified with any single set of philosophical ideas.

It took contemporary inspiration from Husserl's phenomenology, but derived also from various sources in 19th-century philosophy, including Nietzsche and Kierkegaard, whose conception of the 'individual' may be regarded as a prototype for the existentialist view of the human being as solitary, contingent, and self-creating..

Empiricism

Empiricism is a doctrine in the theory of knowledge (epistemology) which stresses the primacy of sense-experience over reason in the acquisition and justification of knowledge. It thus stands opposed to rationalism, and limits a priori knowledge.

Although explicit empiricist notions can be found in medieval philosophy, and perhaps even earlier, its main impetus was gained during the 17th-century revolution in physics, when adherence to empiricist controls was advocated as an antidote to scientifically unproductive metaphysical speculation.

The demand for philosophy to be responsive to the needs of science is a theme that has been invariant through the empiricist tradition from Locke and Hume to Russell and the logical positivists, and is present also in pragmatism.

Logical positivism

Logical positivism is a set of doctrines espoused most famously by a group of philosophers calling themselves the Vienna Circle, who met in Vienna during the 1920s and 1930s.

In the tradition of analytic philosophy and influenced strongly by empiricism and especially by Hume, logical positivism was an attempt to develop empiricist views with the help of logic and mathematics, in particular, in the work of Russell and the young Wittgenstein.

According to logical positivists, sense experience is all we can appeal to in justifying our beliefs or in explaining the meaning of our words. These views give rise to the Verificationist Principle on which the meaning of a sentence is the procedure by which it can be verified.

The logical positivists believed that adoption of their ideas would dissolve all the problems of philosophy because any question to which the answer could not be provided by some experience would be meaningless.

Logical positivism was spread in the UK by Ayer's work and in the USA by the forced emigration of Carnap.

Verificationism

Verificationism (in philosophy) is the view that the meaning of a proposition is its method of verification, the procedure by which its truth or falsity can be determined by observation or experience.

Verificationism was adopted by the logical positivists and was strongly influenced by the empiricist tradition. The verificationist claim resulted in many, if not all, of the propositions of metaphysics being rendered meaningless: as they cannot be verified, they cannot have meaning.

It also resulted in the propositions of mathematics and of logic (which are of course consistent with all observations) being seen as meaningful only in the sense of being tautologies; they tell us nothing and merely show us how things are.

As any non-tautological proposition that cannot be verified by observation is deemed meaningless, this renders all the propositions of ethics and of aesthetics meaningless too, and useful only as expressions of emotion or exclamations.

A major problem for verificationism is that it puts the meaning of all scientific generalizations in jeopardy because these cannot be conclusively verified by observation.

Absolute conception of reality

In his book *Descartes: The Project of Pure Inquiry* (1978), Williams gave a compelling description of the ideal of objectivity in science, which he called the "absolute conception" of reality.

According to this conception, different human perspectives on and representations of the world are the product of interaction between human beings, as constituents of the world, and the world itself as an independently existing reality.

Humans cannot apprehend the world except by some form of perception or representation; yet they can recognize, and to some extent identify and try to compensate for, the distortions or limitations that their own point of view and their relation to the rest of reality introduce.

The aim of objectivity in science is by this method to approach as closely as possible to the absolute conception—a conception of what is there "anyway," independent of the human point of view.

Historical self-consciousness about the contingent elements in this process is compatible with the idea of a single truth toward which humans are trying to make progress.

Williams was cognizant of the doubts that exist regarding whether this ideal is intelligible, let alone attainable, in light of the fact that human thinking must start from some particular historical moment and must use the contingent

27

biological faculties and cultural tools that happen to be at hand. But whatever may be the difficulties in pursuing this ideal, he believed that it makes sense as an ambition.

If there is a way things are anyway, then it makes sense to want to know what that way is and to explain the nature of human perceptions in terms of it.

Morality and the limits of objectivity

Some philosophers, in the tradition of David Hume (1711–76), have denied that there can be objective truth in ethics on the ground that this would have to mean, very implausibly, that moral propositions are true because they represent moral entities or structures that are part of the furniture of the world—moral realities with which humans have some kind of causal interaction, as they do with the physical objects of scientific knowledge.

Williams was also doubtful about objectivity in ethics, but his criticism does not depend on this false analogy with science and is more interesting.

Moral judgments, according to Williams, are about what people should do and how they should live; they do not at all purport to represent how things are in the outside world. So, if there is any objectivity in moral judgments, it would have to be sought in a different analogy with scientific objectivity.

Objective truth in ethics would have to consist not in ethical entities or properties added to the absolute conception of the external world but in the objective validity of the reasoning that supports certain practical, rather than descriptive, judgments about what people should do and how they should live.

28

The analogy with scientific objectivity would reside in the fact that the way to arrive at such objective and universally valid truth would be to detect and correct for the biases and distortions introduced into one's practical judgment by contingencies of one's personal or parochial perspective. The more distortions one could correct, the closer one would get to the truth.

But it is just this aim, central to the idea of moral objectivity that Williams thinks is fundamentally misguided. Williams finds something bizarre about the theoretical ambition of discovering a standard for practical judgment that escapes the perspectival peculiarities of the individual point of view.

This applies to any ethical theory with a strong basis in impartiality or with a claim to universal validity. Williams's basic point is that, in the practical domain, the ambition of transcending one's own point of view is absurd.

If taken seriously, it is likely to be profoundly self-deceived in its application. To Williams, the ambition is akin to that of the person who tries to eliminate from his life all traces of the fact that it is his.

Williams developed this objection through his general view that practical reasons must be "internal" rather than "external": that is, reasons for action must derive from motives that a person already has; they cannot create new motives by themselves, through the force of reason alone.

He also defended a limited form of ethical relativism. He believed that, while there can be ethical truth, it is local and historically contingent and based on reasons deriving from people's actual motives and practices, which are not timeless or universal.

Consequently, moral judgments cannot be applied to cultures too far removed in time and character from the culture in which they originate.

These arguments appear in *Ethics and the Limits of Philosophy* (1985), "A Critique of Utilitarianism" (1973; in *Utilitarianism: For and Against*), and some of the essays reprinted in *Moral Luck* (1981) and *Making Sense of Humanity* (1995).

The debate provoked by Williams's claim that impersonal moral standards undermine the integrity of personal projects and personal relations, which give life its very meaning, was an important part of the moral and political philosophy of the later 20th century.

Even philosophers who did not accept Williams's conclusions were in most cases led to recognize the importance of accommodating the personal point of view as a factor in moral theory.

Williams also raised and explored the deep question of whether a person's moral status is immune to "luck," or purely contingent circumstances, as Kant had argued (for Kant, the moral status of an individual depends only on the quality of his will).

Williams invented the concept of "moral luck" and offered strong reasons to think that people are morally vulnerable to contingencies beyond their control, a conception he found exemplified in Greek tragedy.

Oedipus, for example, is not relieved of guilt for killing his father and marrying his mother by the fact that he did not know at the time that that was what he was doing. Williams's remarkable philosophical-literary-historical work, *Shame and Necessity* (1993), presented these ideas in a rich study of Greek ethical thought.

Williams came to the conclusion that, instead of following the model of natural science, the project of understanding human nature should rely on history, which provides some distance from the perspective of the present without leaving the fullness of the human perspective behind.

During the later part of his career, this viewpoint coincided with his admiration for Nietzsche, whose genealogical method was an example of historical self-exploration.

In Williams's last book, *Truth and Truthfulness* (2002), he applied these ideas to the importance of truth in the theoretical and practical spheres as well as in political and personal relations.

Individualism

Individualism is the term used in political and social philosophy that emphasizes the moral worth of the individual. Although the concept of an individual may seem straightforward, there are many ways of understanding it, both in theory and in practice.

The term individualism itself and its equivalents in other languages, dates— like socialism and other isms— from the 19th century.

Individualism once exhibited interesting national variations, but its various meanings have since largely merged. Following the upheaval of the French Revolution, *individualisme* was used pejoratively in France to signify the sources of social dissolution and anarchy and the elevation of individual interests above those of the collective.

The term's negative connotation was employed by French reactionaries, nationalists, conservatives, liberals, and socialists alike, despite their different views of a feasible and desirable social order.

In Germany, the ideas of individual uniqueness (*Einzigkeit*) and self-realization—in sum, the Romantic notion of individuality—contributed to the cult of individual genius and were later transformed into an organic theory of national community.

According to this view, state and society are not artificial constructs erected on the basis of a social contract but instead unique and self-sufficient cultural wholes. In England, individualism encompassed religious non-conformity (i.e., nonconformity with the Church of England) and economic liberalism in its various versions, including both laissez-faire and moderate state-interventionist approaches.

In the United States, individualism became part of the core American ideology by the 19th century, incorporating the influences of New England Puritanism, Jeffersonianism, and the philosophy of natural rights.

American individualism was Universalist and idealist but acquired a harsher edge as it became infused with elements of social Darwinism (i.e., the survival of the fittest). "Rugged individualism"—extolled by Herbert Hoover during his presidential campaign in 1928—was associated with traditional American values such as personal freedom, capitalism, and limited government.

As James Bryce, British ambassador to the United States (1907–13), wrote in *The American Commonwealth* (1888), "Individualism, the love of enterprise, and the pride in

32

personal freedom have been deemed by Americans not only their choicest, but [their] peculiar and exclusive possession."

The French aristocratic political philosopher Alexis de Tocqueville (1805–59) described individualism in terms of a kind of moderate selfishness that disposed humans to be concerned only with their own small circle of family and friends.

Observing the workings of the American democratic tradition for *Democracy in America* (1835–40), Tocqueville wrote that by leading "each citizen to isolate himself from his fellows and to draw apart with his family and friends," individualism sapped the "virtues of public life," for which civic virtue and association were a suitable remedy.

For the Swiss historian Jacob Burckhardt (1818–97), individualism signified the cult of privacy, which, combined with the growth of self-assertion, had given "impulse to the highest individual development" that flowered in the European Renaissance.

The French sociologist Émile Durkheim (1858–1917) identified two types of individualism: the utilitarian egoism of the English sociologist and philosopher Herbert Spencer (1820–1903), who, according to Durkheim, reduced society to "nothing more than a vast apparatus of production and exchange," and the rationalism of the German philosopher Immanuel Kant (1724–1804), the French philosopher Jean-Jacques Rousseau (1712–1788), and the French Revolution's Declaration of the Rights of Man and of the Citizen (1789), which has as "its primary dogma the autonomy of reason and as its primary rite the doctrine of free enquiry."

33

The Austrian economist F.A. Hayek (1899–1992), who favoured market processes and was distrustful of state intervention, distinguished what he called "false" from "true" individualism.

False individualism, which was represented mainly by French and other continental European writers, is characterized by "an exaggerated belief in the powers of individual reason" and the scope of effective social planning and is "a source of modern socialism"; in contrast, true individualism, whose adherents included John Locke (1632–1704), Bernard de Mandeville (1670–1733), David Hume (1711–76), Adam Ferguson (1723–1816), Adam Smith (1723–90), and Edmund Burke (1729–97), maintained that the "spontaneous collaboration of free men often creates things which are greater than their individual minds can ever fully comprehend" and accepted that individuals must submit "to the anonymous and seemingly irrational forces of society."

Other aspects of individualism pertain to a series of different questions about how to conceive the relation between collectivities and individuals. One such question focuses on how facts about the behaviour of groups, about social processes, and about large-scale historical events are to be explained.

According to methodological individualism, a view advocated by Austrian-born British philosopher Karl Popper (1902–94), any explanation of such a fact ultimately must appeal to, or be stated in terms of, facts about individuals—about their beliefs, desires, and actions.

A closely related view, sometimes called ontological individualism, is the thesis that social or historical groups, processes, and events are nothing more than complexes of individuals and individual actions.

34

Methodological individualism precludes explanations that appeal to social factors that cannot in turn be individualistically explained. Examples are Durkheim's classic account of differential suicide rates in terms of degrees of social integration and the account of the incidence of protest movements in terms of the structure of political opportunities.

Ontological individualism contrasts with various ways of seeing institutions and collectivities as "real"—e.g., the view of corporations or states as agents and the view of bureaucratic roles and rules or status groups as independent of individuals, both constraining and enabling individuals' behaviour.

Another question that arises in debates over individualism is how objects of worth or value (i.e., goods) in moral and political life are to be conceived. Some theorists, known as atomists, argue that no such goods are intrinsically common or communal, maintaining instead that there are only individual goods that accrue to individuals.

According to this perspective, morality and politics are merely the instruments through which each individual attempts to secure such goods for himself. One example of this view is the conception of political authority as ultimately derived from or justified by a hypothetical "contract" between individuals, as in the political philosophy of Thomas Hobbes (1588–1679).

Another is the idea, typical in economics and in other social sciences influenced by economics, that most social institutions and relationships can best be understood by assuming that individual behaviour is motivated primarily by self-interest.

35

Individualism as Tocqueville understood it, with its endorsement of private enjoyments and control of one's personal environment and its neglect of public involvement and communal attachment, has long been lamented and criticized from both the right and the left and from both religious and secular perspectives.

Especially notable critiques have been made by advocates of communitarianism, who tend to equate individualism with narcissism and selfishness.

Likewise, thinkers in the tradition of "republican" political thought—according to which power is best controlled by being divided—are disturbed by their perception that individualism deprives the state of the support and active involvement of citizens, thereby impairing democratic institutions.

Individualism also has been thought to distinguish modern Western societies from pre-modern and non-Western ones, such as traditional India and China, where, it is said, the community or the nation is valued above the individual and an individual's role in the political and economic life of his community is largely determined by his membership in a specific class or caste.

Branches of Philosophy and Stoicism

Philosophy

Philosophy (Greek, 'love of wisdom'), the use of reason and argument in the search for truth and the nature of reality, especially of the causes and nature of things and of the principles governing existence, perception, human behaviour, and the material universe.

Philosophical activities can also be directed at understanding and clarifying the concepts, methods, and doctrines of other disciplines, or at reasoning itself (philosophical logic) and the concepts, methods, and doctrines of such general notions as truth, possibility, knowledge (epistemology), necessity, existence (ontology and metaphysics), and proof.

Philosophy has many different areas, classified according to the subject-matter of the problems being addressed, thus:

- Philosophy of mind is concerned with questions such as 'how does the mental interact with the physical?';

- Philosophy of mathematics with questions such as 'what constitutes a proof?';

- Religion ('does God exist?');

- Science ('what constitutes good evidence for a hypothesis?');

- Ethics;

- Politics; and

- Indeed of any other discipline.

37

The first philosophers were also the first scientists, people who asked questions about the physical world and who attempted to answer them by observation and reasoning rather than by appealing to magic or to a God of some kind.

These people, known as the pre-Socratics, were the precursors of Socrates, Plato, and Aristotle, the three great philosophers who set the agenda for many of the philosophical questions debated today.

Philosophy regularly gives birth to new disciplines as one group of the questions it is trying to answer become amenable to study by the physical sciences.

Psychology, for example, is a discipline that is still in the process of separating itself from philosophy. Great advances in scientific thinking have usually been accompanied by great advances in philosophical thinking.

For example, Galileo's work on the mechanics of planetary motion in the late 16th century was a motivating force in Descartes's work on knowledge and justification, while the physicist Albert Einstein (1879-1955) paid tribute to Hume as one of the philosophers whose work inspired his theory of relativity.

In the 20th century, the principal schools of philosophy are continental philosophy and logico-analytic philosophy. Within these principal schools, however, there are major divisions according to sides taken in the various great disputes of philosophy.

For example, until fairly recently it was a matter of great concern whether someone was a dualist or a monist-- whether they believed that there are two different sorts of substance (the physical and the mental), or only one sort-- either the physical (materialism) or the mental.

There are also major disputes about whether or not there are such things as 'innate ideas', concepts that are inborn rather than acquired through experience, and whether we can make sense of a world that is independent of us and our minds (realism) or whether the mind is in fact more fundamental than some extra-mental reality (idealism).

Rather than being empirical scientists, philosophers try to discern the logical form of the problems in which they are interested and to discover hidden fallacies or habits of mind which might be obscuring understanding.

The only experiments indulged in by philosophers are thought experiments. The interpretation of various doctrines in modern physics is currently of great interest to philosophers: at least one interpretation of the laws of quantum physics would invalidate some of the rules of classical logic.

Moreover, advances in engineering, computing and psychology have brought us close to the production of an artificial intelligence, a fact of interest not only to philosophers of mind, but one that introduces ethical questions of great importance.

Major areas in which philosophy can be applied to the problems of everyday life are moral and political philosophy, especially in medical ethics such as the prevention of conception and the enhancement of fertility.

In such cases very deep moral problems arise, the solutions to which require sustained and critical examination of what is right and what is wrong. These investigations are usually carried out by interdisciplinary committees in which philosophers play a major part.

Metaphysics

Metaphysics (from Greek, 'the things after the physics', from the ordering of Aristotle's works) is that branch of philosophy which studies the most general categories and concepts which are presupposed in descriptions of ourselves and the world. Examples are causality, substance, ontology, time, and reality.

Metaphysical questions have a very broad scope.

- Whereas the physical scientist might ask 'How does x cause y?',

- The metaphysician asks 'What does it mean for anything to cause anything else?'.

- Whereas the chemist might investigate particular substances, the metaphysician asks what it means to be a substance, and whether there is one basic substance, or many.

Metaphysical questions can become the subject of more specialized philosophical inquiry. We can ask whether our actions are subject to causality, which gives rise to the problem of free will. The question of whether our mental experiences involve a separate substance from body is a major issue in the philosophy of mind.

Although metaphysics dates back to the ancient Greeks, there have been occasions on which its status as a legitimate inquiry have been questioned.

The rise of science in the 17th century led to attempts by philosophers such as Hume and Locke to limit the claims of metaphysics, and earlier this century scientifically minded philosophers such as the logical positivists claimed that metaphysical assertions were meaningless.

Epistemology

Epistemology is the philosophical theory of knowledge.

It is generally assumed that the difference between a belief which makes a genuine claim to knowledge, and one which is a mere statement of opinion, is that the former can some-how be justified.

Epistemology can be regarded as the investigation of what constitutes that justification, and how, or whether, it can be attained. Scepticism is the position which holds that justification, and hence knowledge, is not possible.

Traditionally conflicting theories about knowledge have been rationalism, which claims that ultimate justification for our beliefs is to be found in reason and empiricism, which argues that it is to be found in our sense-experiences. The traditional debate, then, has concerned the nature of the foundation of knowledge.

More recently, however, attention has been focused on the structure of knowledge, that is, how our true beliefs are related to one another.

The assumption that knowledge has to have a starting-point in any sort of foundation has been questioned by the Coherence Theory of Knowledge, which suggests, instead, that a belief is justified to the extent to which it fits in, or coheres with, all our other beliefs.

Major contributors to stoicism

Zeno

Zeno of Citium (*c.*335-*c.*262 BC), Greek philosopher. He was the founder of the Stoics. He attended the Academy in Athens, devoting himself first to the Cynic philosophy and then to the Socratic method of enquiry.

The school of thought which he originated included a theory of knowledge, ethics, and physics, and a new system of logic.

He taught that virtue, the one true good, is the only important thing, the virtue of a wise man cannot be destroyed, and that the vicissitudes of life are irrelevant to a man's happiness.

Cato

Cato, Marcus Porcius (the Younger) (95-46 BC), the great-grandson of Cato the Elder. He was known posthumously as 'Uticensis' after the place of his death.

A conservative republican, he long opposed Pompey, but finally sided with him against Julius Caesar. He committed suicide at Utica in northern Africa after Caesar's victory at Thapsus rather than seek Caesar's pardon.

Less noteworthy than his great-grandfather, he nevertheless became proverbial as an exemplar of republican and traditional Roman values.

Brutus

Brutus, Marcus Junius (*c*.85-42 BC), Roman soldier, one of the assassins of Julius Caesar. He was the nephew of Cato and a conservative republican Roman.

He took Pompey's side against Caesar in the Roman civil wars. Pardoned by Caesar after Pharsalus, he became governor of Cisalpine Gaul, and then urban praetor in 44 through Caesar's favour.

Together with Cassius he plotted Caesar's death. It was Brutus' idealism which confined the conspirators' action to the single act of killing Caesar: they thereby lost the political initiative to the consul Antony, whom they had spared, and were compelled to flee, afterwards forming a fleet and army in Greece against Mark Antony and Octavian.

Defeat at Philippi in 42 was followed by his suicide.

Cicero

Cicero, Marcus Tullius (106-43 BC), Roman orator, statesman, and philosopher. He first made his name as a lawyer in civil and criminal trials. His brilliant prosecution of Verres, the corrupt Roman governor of Sicily, in 70, established his reputation and the nobility came to see in him a strong candidate for the consulship of 63.

As consul he outmanoeuvred Catiline and his fellow conspirators, who were plotting to take over Rome. He spoke out against the First Triumvirate, and was exiled on the charge of executing the Cataline conspirators without trial.

The exertions of his friends secured his recall in 57 amid popular acclaim. He returned to Rome just before the eruption of civil war, which he did his best to avert. His allegiance lay with Pompey and the senatorial cause but he became disillusioned by Pompey's leadership and after his defeat at Pharsalus, returned to Italy.

Caesar admired him greatly and valued his political support but he rejected Caesar and immersed himself in his philosophical writings. After Caesar's assassination it fell to Cicero to rally the Senate. He denounced Mark Antony in the *Philippicae* ('Philippic Orations') and hoped that he could revive the republic. In 43 Antony, Octavian, and Lepidus ordered him to be put to death and he was captured and killed.

Although Cicero rated his political role most highly his lasting claim to greatness rests on his writings. Cicero was fascinated by the theory as well as the practice of oratory and its branches, such as rhetoric, and in a series of works expounded the principles of the art.

No one, apart from himself, much admired Cicero's poetry; but his letters, especially those to his friend Atticus, which were not meant for publication, give an unrivalled view of contemporary Roman politics and social life, in a style of brilliant variety and vigour. No less remarkable is a series of philosophical works, written as a consolation during years of political inactivity.

They are largely based on Greek sources, but, with their dialogue form (based on Plato), they bring to life the basic philosophical quarrel between hedonistic Epicureans and rigorous Stoics.

Cicero found Latin a language ill-suited to abstract exposition and it is an important part of his achievement that he greatly expanded its vocabulary and developed a fluent and adaptable style that enabled the Christian writers

44

of the 4th century to expound and forward the doctrines of their faith. He has remained an influence on Western thought and literature to this day.

Aurelius

Marcus Aurelius, (AD 121-80) was a Roman emperor (161-80) and Stoic philosopher.

He was born of Spanish parents, and adopted as Hadrian's grandson.

A student of literature, philosophy, and law, his succession to the imperial title in 161 plunged him into military activity on frontiers in the Balkans, Dacia, Pannonia, and Syria.

His 'Meditations', largely written on campaign, survive with some of his letters. While an admirer of Epictetus, he persecuted the Christians.

Epictetus

Epictetus (*c.* AD 50-135), Phrygian Stoic philosopher. He was expelled from Rome *c.*90 AD when Emperor Domitian proscribed all philosophers.

Although he wrote nothing himself, the lecture notes taken by the historian Arrian, survived him. He was contemporary with the rise of Christianity and his Stoicism, combined with a strong belief in one God, has many similarities with the teaching of Jesus Christ.

He insisted that trust in God was the only answer to the mysteries of pain, loss, and death. Marcus Aurelius admired him greatly.

Aristotle

Aristotle (384-322 BC), one of the most celebrated Greek philosophers. At the age of 17 he joined Plato's Academy, where he stayed until shortly after Plato's death in 347. He was later (343-2) appointed tutor to Alexander the Great.

In 335 he returned to Athens, where he established a school and a collection of manuscripts which was the model for later libraries. He organised research projects, the fruit of one being a comparative study of 158 Greek constitutions. Following the death of Alexander in 323, he was charged with impiety and left Athens, dying soon afterwards in Chalcis.

His output was enormous and survives largely in the form of notes for lectures delivered at the Lyceum, successor to Plato's Academy. Aristotle's work encompasses dialogues which exist only in fragments:

- Collections of historical information;

- Extant *Constitution of the Athenians* (though the authorship of this is now doubted);

- Scientific and philosophical works which are mostly extant, such as the *Nicomachaean Ethics*, the *Politics*,

- *Metaphysics*, some of which reveal the influence of Plato.

These writings reveal the encyclopaedic nature of Aristotle's interests and his logical, carefully organized work laid the foundations of many later philosophical enquiries. He introduced the systematic study of logic, developing a system for describing and assessing reasoning that remained the core of the discipline until the 19th century.

Contemporary categorial grammar can be traced to Aristotle's interest in the functioning of words, giving him a special place in philosophical logic and in linguistics.

The central questions of Aristotle's *Metaphysics* (What is substance?) and his *On Coming to be and Passing Away* (How do things come into existence and cease to exist?) are still hotly debated. In *De Anima* (On the Soul) Aristotle discussed the soul, or psyche; that which makes something alive and capable of the activities characteristic of life.

In claiming that the psyche is dependent upon the body, Aristotle anticipated the mind/body debate current in philosophy of mind. Contemporary ethics also owes a debt to Aristotle's *Ethics*. His claim that all action aims at *eudaimonia*, or happiness, seemingly has much in common with modern-day utilitarianism; however, Aristotle's stress on the several virtues is in tension with utilitarianism's promise of a single (if not simple) principle for deciding all moral questions.

Aristotle's work was rediscovered by Arab scholars, notably Avicenna and Averroes, and, translated into Latin, shaped the development of medieval thought in the arts and sciences. St Thomas Aquinas reconciled the Aristotelian doctrines with those of Christian theology and they remained a key part of higher education in Europe from the 13th to the 17th centuries.

Scope of Stoicism

Stoicism

Stoicism is a school of thought that flourished in Greek and Roman antiquity.

It was one of the loftiest and most sublime philosophies in the record of Western civilization.

In urging participation in human affairs, Stoics have always believed that the goal of all inquiry is to provide a mode of conduct characterized by tranquillity of mind and certainty of moral worth.

Nature and scope of Stoicism

For the early Stoic philosopher, as for all the post-Aristotelian schools, knowledge and its pursuit are no longer held to be ends in themselves.

The Hellenistic Age was a time of transition, and the Stoic philosopher was perhaps its most influential spokesman. A new culture was in the making. The heritage of an earlier period, with Athens as its intellectual leader, was to continue, but to undergo many changes.

If, as with Socrates, to know is to know oneself, rationality as the sole means by which something outside of the self might be achieved may be said to be the hallmark of Stoic belief.

As a Hellenistic philosophy, Stoicism presented an *ars vitae*, a way of accommodation for people to whom the human condition no longer appeared as the mirror of a universal, calm, and ordered existence.

Reason alone could reveal the constancy of cosmic order and the originative source of unyielding value; thus, reason became the true model for human existence.

To the Stoic, virtue is an inherent feature of the world, no less inexorable in relation to humans than are the laws of nature.

The Stoics believed that perception is the basis of true knowledge. In logic, their comprehensive presentation of the topic is derived from perception, yielding not only the judgment that knowledge is possible but also that certainty is possible, on the analogy of the incorrigibility of perceptual experience. To them, the world is composed of material things, with some few exceptions (e.g., meaning), and the irreducible element in all things is right reason, which pervades the world as divine fire.

Things, such as material, or corporeal, bodies, are governed by this reason or fate, in which virtue is inherent. The world in its awesome entirety is so ruled as to exhibit grandeur of orderly arrangement that can only serve as a standard for humankind in the regulation and ordering of life.

Thus, the goal of humans is to live according to nature, in agreement with the world design. Stoic moral theory is also based on the view that the world, as one great city, is a unity.

Humans, as world citizens, have an obligation and loyalty to all things in that city. They must play an active role in world affairs, remembering that the world exemplifies virtue and right action.

Thus, moral worth, duty, and justice are singularly Stoic emphases, together with a certain sternness of mind. For the moral person neither is merciful nor shows pity, because each suggests a deviation from duty and from the fated necessity that rules the world.

Nonetheless—with its loftiness of spirit and its emphasis on the individual's essential worth—the themes of universal brotherhood and the benevolence of divine nature make Stoicism one of the most appealing of philosophies.

Its chief competitors in antiquity were:

    (1) Epicureanism, with its doctrine of a life of withdrawal in contemplation and escape from worldly affairs and its belief that pleasure, as the absence of pain, is the goal of humans;

    (2) Scepticism, which rejected certain knowledge in favour of local beliefs and customs, in the expectation that these guides would provide the quietude and serenity that the dogmatic philosopher (e.g., the Stoic) could not hope to achieve; and

    (3) Christianity, with its hope of personal salvation provided by an appeal to faith as an immanent aid to human understanding and by the beneficent intervention of a merciful God.

Along with its rivals, Stoicism enabled the individual to better order his own life and to avoid the excesses of human nature that promote disquietude and anxiety.

It was easily the most influential of the schools from the time of its founding through the first two centuries CE, and it continued to have a marked effect on later thought.

During the late Roman and medieval periods, elements of Stoic moral theory were known and used in the formulation of Christian, Jewish, and Islamic theories of humanity and nature, of the state and society, and of law and sanctions— e.g., in the works of Cicero, Roman statesman and orator; in Lactantius, often called the "Christian Cicero"; and in Boethius, a scholar transitional to the Middle Ages.

In the Renaissance, Stoic political and moral theory became more popular to theorists of natural law and political authority and of educational reform—e.g., in Hugo Grotius, a Dutch jurist and statesman, and in Philipp Melanchthon, a major Reformation scholar.

In the 20th century, Stoicism became popular again for its insistence on the value of the individual and the place of value in a world of strife and uncertainty—e.g., in existentialism and in Neo-orthodox Protestant theology.

Stoicism also played an important role in reassessments of the history of logic—e.g., in Jan Łukasiewicz, a Polish logician, and in William and Martha Kneale, mid-20th-century British logicians.

Greek Stoicism

With the death of Aristotle (322 BCE) and that of Alexander the Great (323 BCE), the greatness of the life and thought of the Greek city-state (polis) ended.

With Athens no longer the centre of worldly attraction, its claim to urbanity and cultural prominence passed on to other cities—to Rome, to Alexandria, and to Pergamum. The Greek polis gave way to larger political units; local rule was replaced by that of distant governors.

The earlier distinction between Greek and barbarian was destroyed; provincial and tribal loyalties were broken apart, first by Alexander and then by Roman legions.

The loss of freedom by subject peoples further encouraged a deterioration of the concept of the freeman and resulted in the rendering of obligation and service to a ruler whose moral force held little meaning.

The earlier intimacy of order, cosmic and civic, was now replaced by social and political disorder; and traditional mores gave way to uncertain and transient values.

Stoicism had its beginnings in a changing world, in which earlier codes of conduct and ways of understanding proved no longer suitable. But it was also influenced by tenets of the older schools.

The earliest Greek philosophers, the Milesians, had called attention to cosmic order and the beauty of nature. Later, the monist Parmenides of Elea stressed the power of reason and thought, whereas Heracleitus of Ephesus, precursor of the philosophy of becoming, had alluded to the constancy of change and the omnipresence of divine fire, which illumined all things.

A deeper understanding of human nature came with Socrates, symbol of the philosopher, who personified *sophia* and *sapientia* (Greek and Latin: "wisdom").

Of the several schools of philosophy stemming from Socrates, the Cynic and Megarian schools were influential in the early development of Stoic doctrine: the Cynics for their emphasis on the simple life, unadorned and free of emotional involvement; and the Megarians for their study of dialectic, logical form, and paradoxes.

Stoicism takes its name from the place where its founder, Zeno of Citium (Cyprus), customarily lectured—the Stoa Poikile (Painted Colonnade). Zeno, who flourished in the early 3rd century BCE, showed in his own doctrines the influence of earlier Greek attitudes, particularly those mentioned above. He was apparently well versed in Platonic thought, for he had studied at Plato's Academy both with Xenocrates of Chalcedon and with Polemon of Athens, successive heads of the Academy.

Zeno was responsible for the division of philosophy into three parts:

1. Logic,

2. Physics, and

3. Ethics.

He also established the central Stoic doctrines in each part, so that later Stoics were to expand rather than to change radically the views of the founder.

With some exceptions (in the field of logic), Zeno thus provided the following themes as the essential framework of Stoic philosophy:

- Logic as an instrument and not as an end in itself;

- Human happiness as a product of life according to nature;

- Physical theory as providing the means by which right actions are to be determined;

- Perception as the basis of certain knowledge;

- Wise person as the model of human excellence;

- Platonic forms—the abstract entities in which things of the same genus "participate"—as being unreal;

- True knowledge as always accompanied by assent;

- the fundamental substance of all existing things as being a divine fire, the universal principles of which are:

    (1) Passive (matter) and

    (2) Active (reason inherent in matter);

    - Belief in a world conflagration and renewal;

    - Belief in the corporeality of all things;

    - Belief in the fated causality that necessarily binds all things;

    - Cosmopolitanism, or cultural outlook transcending narrower loyalties;

    - Obligation, or duty, to choose only those acts that are in accord with nature, all other acts being a matter of indifference.

Cleanthes of Assos, who succeeded Zeno as head of the school, is best known for his *Hymn to Zeus,* which movingly describes Stoic reverence for the cosmic order and the power of universal reason and law.

The third head of the school, Chrysippus of Soli, who lived to the end of the 3rd century, was perhaps the greatest and certainly the most productive of the early Stoics.

He devoted his considerable energies to the almost complete development of the Zenonian themes in logic, physics, and ethics. In logic particularly, he defended against the

Megarian logicians and the Sceptics such concepts as certain knowledge, comprehensive presentation, proposition and argument, truth and its criterion, and assent.

His work in propositional logic, in which unanalyzed propositions joined by connectives are studied, made important contributions to the history of ancient logic and is of particular relevance to more recent developments in logic.

In physics, Chrysippus was responsible for the attempt to show that fate and free will are not mutually exclusive conceptual features of Stoic doctrine. He further distinguished between "whole" and "all," or "universe," arguing that the whole is the world, while the all is the external void together with the world.

Zeno's view of the origin of human beings as providentially generated by "fiery reason" out of matter was expanded by Chrysippus to include the concept of self-preservation, which governs all living things.

Another earlier view (Zeno's), that of nature as a model for life, was amplified first by Cleanthes and then by Chrysippus. The Zenonian appeal to life "according to nature" had evidently been left vague, because to Cleanthes it seemed necessary to speak of life in accord with nature conceived as the world at large (the cosmos), whereas Chrysippus distinguished between world nature and human nature.

Thus, to do good is to act in accord with both human and universal nature. Chrysippus also expanded the Stoic view that seminal reasons were the impetus for animate motion. He established firmly that logic and (especially) physics are necessary and are means for the differentiation of goods and evils.

55

Thus, knowledge of physics (or theology) is required before an ethics can be formulated. Indeed, physics and logic find their value chiefly in this very purpose. Chrysippus covered almost every feature of Stoic doctrine and treated each so thoroughly that the essential features of the school were to change relatively little after his time.

Roman Stoicism

The Middle Stoa, which flourished in the 2nd and early 1st centuries BCE, was dominated chiefly by two philosophers of Rhodes: Panaetius, its founder, and his disciple Poseidonius.

Panaetius organized a Stoic school in Rome before returning to Athens, and Poseidonius was largely responsible for an emphasis on the religious features of the doctrine.

Both were antagonistic to the ethical doctrines of Chrysippus, who, they believed, had strayed too far from the Platonic and Aristotelian roots of Stoicism. It may have been because of the considerable time that Panaetius and Poseidonius lived in Rome that the Stoa there turned so much of its emphasis to the moral and religious themes within the Stoic doctrine.

Panaetius was highly regarded by Cicero, who used him as a model for his own work. Poseidonius, who had been a disciple of Panaetius in Athens, taught Cicero at his school at Rhodes and later went to Rome and remained there for a time with Cicero.

If Poseidonius admired Plato and Aristotle, he was particularly interested—unlike most of his school—in the study of natural and providential phenomena. In presenting

56

the Stoic system in the second book of *De natura deorum* (45 BCE; *On the Nature of the Gods*), Cicero most probably followed Poseidonius.

Because his master, Panaetius, was chiefly concerned with concepts of duty and obligation, it was his studies that served as a model for the *De officiis* (44 BCE; *On Duties*) of Cicero. Hecaton, another of Panaetius's students and an active Stoic philosopher, also stressed similar ethical themes.

If Chrysippus is to be commended for his diligence in defending Stoic logic and epistemology against the Scepticism of the New Academy (3rd–2nd century BCE), it was chiefly Panaetius and Poseidonius who were responsible for the widespread popularity of Stoicism in Rome.

It was precisely their turning of doctrine to themes in moral philosophy and natural science that appealed to the intensely practical Romans. The times perhaps demanded such interests, and with them Stoicism was to become predominantly a philosophy for the individual, showing how—given the vicissitudes of life—one might be stoical.

Law, world citizenship, nature, and the benevolent workings of providence and the divine reason were the principal areas of interest of Stoicism at this time.

These tendencies toward practicality are also well illustrated in the later period of the school (in the first two centuries CE) in the writings of Lucius Seneca, a Roman statesman; of Epictetus, a former slave; and of Marcus Aurelius, a Roman emperor. Both style and content in Seneca's *Libri morales* (*Moral Essays*) and *Epistulae morales* (*Moral Letters*) reinforce the new direction in Stoic thought.

The *Encheiridion* (*Manual*) of Epictetus and the *Meditations* of Marcus Aurelius furthered the sublime and yet personal consolation of the Stoic message and increasingly showed the strength of its rivalry to the burgeoning power of the new Christianity.

The mark of a guide, of the religious teacher, is pre-eminent in these writings. It is difficult to establish with any precision, however, the extent of Stoic influence by the time of the first half of the 2nd century CE.

So popular had these ideas become that many specifically Stoic terms (viz., *right reason, comprehension, assent, indifference, logos,* and *natural law*), as well as the notion of the wise person, commonly were used in debate and intellectual disputes.

Stoic elements

There is much disagreement as to the measure of Stoic influence on the writings of St. Paul the Apostle. At Tarsus, Paul certainly had opportunities for hearing Stoic lectures on philosophy.

It may be that his discussion of nature and the teaching of it (1 Corinthians 11:14) is Stoic in origin, for it has a parallel in the *Manual* of Epictetus 1.16, 10. Although not a Stoic technical term, *syneidēsis,* which Paul used as "conscience," was generally employed by Stoic philosophers.

In 1 Corinthians 13 and in the report of Paul's speech at Athens (Acts 17), there is much that is Hellenistic, more than a little tinged by Stoic elements—e.g., the arguments concerning the natural belief in God and the belief that human existence is in God.

The assimilation of Stoic elements by the Church Fathers was generally better understood by the 4th century. Stoic influence can be seen, for example, in the relation between reason and the passions in the works of St. Ambrose, one of the great scholars of the church, and of Marcus Minucius Felix, a Christian Apologist. Each took a wealth of ideas from Stoic morality as Cicero had interpreted it in *De officiis*.

In general, whereas the emerging Christian morality affirmed its originality, it also assimilated much of the pagan literature, the more congenial elements of which were essentially Stoic.

Earlier, in the 3rd century, Quintus Tertullian, often called the father of Latin Christian literature, seems to have been versed in Stoic philosophy—e.g., in his theory of the agreement between the supernatural and the human soul, in his use of the Stoic tenet that from a truth there follow truths, and in his employment of the idea of universal consent.

Even in his polemical writings, which reveal an unrelenting hostility to pagan philosophy, Tertullian showed a fundamental grasp and appreciation of such Stoic themes as the world logos and the relation of body to soul.

This is well illustrated in his argument against the Stoics, particularly on their theme that God is a corporeal being and identified with reason as inherent in matter—also to be found in his polemics against Marcion, father of a heretical Christian sect (the Marcionites), and against Hermogenes of Tarsus, author of an important digest of rhetoric.

Yet in his doctrine of the Word, he appealed directly to Zeno and Cleanthes of the Early Stoa. Another important polemic against the Stoics is found in the treatise *Contra Celsum,* by Origen, the most influential Greek theologian of the 3rd century, in which he argued at some length against Stoic doctrines linking God to matter.

Also, St. Cyprian, bishop of Carthage in the 3rd century, revealed the currency of Stoic views—e.g., in his *Ad Demetrianum* (*To Demetrius*), a denunciation of an enemy to Christianity, in which Cyprian castigates the ill treatment of slaves, who, no less than their masters, are formed of the same matter and endowed with the same soul and live according to the same law.

The beliefs in human brotherhood and in the world as a great city, commonly found in early Christian literature, were current Stoic themes. The Christian attitude appears in what St. Paul said of Baptism: "You are all sons of God through Faith. For as many of you as were baptized into Christ have put on Christ" (Galatians 3:26–27).

Stoic undercurrents in medieval thought

During the period when Christian institutions and doctrines were developing (230–1450 CE), Stoicism continued to play a popular role. The *De consolatione philosophiae* (524; *Consolation of Philosophy*) of Boethius (died 524/525 CE) was widely known and appreciated as a discourse on the mysterious questions of the nature of good and evil, of fortune, chance, or freedom, and of divine foreknowledge.

If the plan of Boethius was to serve as an interpreter of Plato and Aristotle, he succeeded only in working through some logical theories of Aristotle, together with several commentaries on those theories.

In the *Consolatione*, however, the themes are quite different; in the fifth book; for example, he attempted to resolve the apparent difficulty of reconciling human freedom (free will) with the divine foreknowledge, a problem that among Stoic thinkers—though by no means uniquely among them—had been in general currency for a long time.

This work of emancipation from worldly travail through the glories of reason and philosophy, which included Stoic doctrines as found in the writings of Cicero and Seneca, was much more influential for later medieval thought than that of Lactantius, of the late 3rd to early 4th century, who was largely concerned with the writing of a history of religion—a summary statement of Christian doctrine and life from earliest times.

Lactantius also wrote a not unimportant work called *De ira Dei* (313; *On the Anger of God*). It poses a problem of how to deal with the essentially Greek, or philosophical, view that God cannot feel anger because he is not subject to passions and that *apatheia* ("apathy," or "imperturbableness") is not merely the mark of the wise person but also a divine attribute.

This view, which had been most thoroughly developed among Stoic thinkers and particularly by Epictetus, raised a peculiarly Christian problem, the concern of the power of God to reward the righteous and punish the transgressor; thus, it challenged the very idea of providence.

Other manifestations of anthropopathism, the attributing of human feelings to God, had also been charged against the early Christian religionists; and the writers of the time—Lactantius and Tertullian among them—took great pains to refute the largely Stoic formulations of these charges.

Although the refutations took the form—in St. Augustine, for example—of denying that the wrath of God is a perturbation of the soul and of holding that it is rather a judgment, the concept of the divine essence excludes all passions.

Within the monastic tradition, there remained more than a residue of concern over apathy as a divine attribute and as a model for the truly religious.

Other significant Stoic influences appeared in medieval discussions of the popular origin of political authority and of the distinctions made in law between *jus naturale* (natural law), *jus gentium* (law of nations), *jus civile* (civil law)— doctrines of Stoic origin—found in 3rd-century Roman juridical texts gathered together by St. Isidore of Sevilla (died 636 CE), a Spanish encyclopaedist and theologian.

The Stoic belief—as against Aristotle—that humans are by nature equal was an integral part of the knowledge that certain rules of law are universally recognized, laws that all people might naturally follow.

In this way, the Romans—whose genius lay in organization and in law—fostered the conception of natural, or common, law, which reason was supposed to make evident to all people.

Thus, in the second half of the 11th century, the Stoic texts of Cicero and Seneca became important doctrinal sources for the initial discussions of social and political philosophy.

These early theories of law, of natural equality, and of the rights of prince and populace were to become the basis for 13th-century systems of social and political privilege and obligation.

In the 12th century, John of Salisbury, an English critical scholar, produced, in his *Policraticus* (1159), the first complete attempt at a philosophy of the state since Classical times.

62

Stoic doctrines of natural law, society, state, and providence were important elements in his effort to construct a social philosophy on ethical and metaphysical principles.

The impact of these doctrines and the lengthy history of their use in the earlier Middle Ages can also be found in the views of St. Thomas Aquinas on the philosophy of the state and of human nature.

Renascence of Stoicism

If the influence of Stoic doctrines during the Middle Ages was largely restricted to the resolution of problems of social and political significance, it remained for the Renaissance, in its passion for the rediscovery of Greek and Roman antiquity, to provide a basis for the rebirth of Stoic views in logic, epistemology, and metaphysics, as well as the documentation of the more familiar Stoic doctrines in ethics and politics.

Late in the 16th century, Justus Lipsius, a Flemish scholar and Latin humanist, was responsible for the first restatement of Stoicism as a defensible and thoroughgoing (Christian) philosophy of human nature.

His treatises *De constantia* (1584; *On Constancy*) and *Politicorum sive civilis doctrinae libri sex* (1589; *Six Books of Politics or Political Instruction*) were widely known in many editions and translations.

His defence of Stoic doctrine in *Manuductio ad Stoicam Philosophiam* (1604; *Digest of Stoic Philosophy*) and *Physiologia Stoicorum* (1604; *Physics of the Stoics*) provided the basis for the considerable Stoic influence during the Renaissance.

63

About the turn of the 17th century, Guillaume du Vair, a French lawyer and Christian philosopher, made Stoic moral philosophy popular, while Pierre Charron, a French theologian and sceptic, utilized Stoic themes in *De la sagesse* (1601; *Of Wisdom*), as did the skeptic Michel de Montaigne in his *Essais* (1580).

Through the work of Lipsius, Stoic doctrines were to influence the thought of Francis Bacon, a precursor of modern philosophy of science, and, later, the *De l'esprit des lois* (1748; *The Spirit of Laws*), by the political theorist Charles-Louis, baron de Montesquieu.

In the continuing and relentless war against the Aristotelianism of the later Middle Ages, the doctrines of Stoicism influenced many prominent figures of the Renaissance and Reformation periods.

Pietro Pomponazzi, an Aristotelian of early 16th-century Italy, in defending an anti-Scholastic Aristotelianism against the Averroists, who viewed the world as a strictly necessitarian and fated order, adopted the Stoic view of providence and human freedom.

The 15th-century humanist Leonardo Bruni absorbed Stoic views on reason, fate, and free will. Pantheism, the view that God and nature are unitary in the sense that God is an impersonal being, and naturalism, the view that nothing is supernatural, both of which identify God with the cosmos and ascribe to it a life process of which the world soul is the principle, were widely held Renaissance notions.

Such a pantheistic naturalism was advocated—though from diverse standpoints—by Francesco Patrizi, a versatile Platonist, and by Giordano Bruno, defender of an infinite cosmos; and in both authors the inspiration and source were fundamentally Stoic.

In the development of a philosophy of public law based upon a study of human nature, Stoic elements are found in the *Utopia* (1516), by Thomas More, and the *De Jure Belli ac Pacis* (1625; *On the Law of War and Peace*), by Hugo Grotius. This latter work is one of the most famous Renaissance treatises on the theory of natural and social rights.

The foremost Swiss reformer of the early 16th century, Huldrych Zwingli, who regarded justification by subjective belief as the foundation of the new Christianity, utilized Stoic views on the autonomy of the will, on the absolute predestination of the good and evil person, and on moral determinism.

Another Stoic influence of considerable importance in the tradition of Christian humanism was the view that all religions have a common basis of truths concerning God—a universal Deism. Among those who favoured such a view were Zwingli and Desiderius Erasmus, the great Renaissance humanist and scholar.

More and Grotius also laid special stress on this view, and its influence was felt in the moral, social, and even the artistic life of the 16th century. Later, Herbert of Cherbury, often called the father of Deism, further developed the idea of religious peace and the reduction of opposing religious views to common elements. This view became one of the most popular ideas of the 17th century.

Philipp Melanchthon also cultivated humanism and the philosophy of antiquity as a basis for a reborn Christianity. Although Aristotle was his chief inspiration, Melanchthon made telling use of the Stoic theory of knowledge, with its notions of innate principles and the natural light of reason, which teach the great truths of metaphysical and moral order.

Stoicism thus became the basis for the natural-law theory, which holds that the state is of immediately divine origin and independent of the church—a Protestant view opposed by Roman Catholic writers.

The Cartesian revolution in thought in the 17th century brought forward several Stoic notions, that:

- Morality consists of obedience to the law of reason, which God has deposited within humans;

- Ethics presupposes a knowledge of nature, because humans must learn to know their place in the world, for only then may they act rightly;

- Self-examination is the foundation of ethics; and that

- Innateness and commonality of truths bespeak the view that only thoughts and the will belong properly to humans, for the body is a part of the material world.

Such views were particularly developed by René Descartes, often hailed as the father of modern philosophy, in his dualism of mind (or soul) and body.

Benedict de Spinoza, a freethinking Jewish rationalist, made similar use of Stoic views on the nature of humans and the world. That aspect of Spinoza's thought that is debatably labelled pantheist is essentially Stoic in character.

Together with the Cartesians, Spinoza insisted upon the importance of internal and right reason as the sole means by which to attain to indubitable truths and to the possibility of human freedom.

Blaise Pascal, a French scientist and religious writer, also was sympathetic to Cartesian conceptions of human nature.

Though he turned his back on philosophy, his religious thought retained the Cartesian and Stoic insistence on the independence of human reason, holding that humans are fundamentally thinking beings, innately capable of making right decisions.

There is an important and crucial difference and conflict between Pascal's views and those of Spinoza and the Cartesians: for Pascal, though the use of (the Stoic) right reason might result in proofs and demonstrations that lead to the God of truth, it would never lead to the God of love, the one true God.

Thus, the Stoic exaltation of reason to an entity in its own right—indeed, to a divine entity—as exemplified among the Cartesians and in the thought of Spinoza, was rejected by Pascal in the Jansenist Christianity that he finally adopted— a rejection that, because it also repudiated free will, distinguishes Pascal from those who held Stoic as well as alternative conceptions of human freedom and responsibility.

Christianity in general, in spite of striking contrasts with Stoicism, has found elements within it that parallel its own position. As the Stoic, for example, feels safe and protected in the rational care of some immanent providence, so the Christian senses that a transcendent though incarnate and loving God is looking after him.

In general, Stoicism has played a great part throughout the ages in the theological formulation of Christian thought as well as in the actual realization of the Christian ideals.

Contemporary philosophy has borrowed from Stoicism, at least in part, its conviction that human beings must be conceived as being closely and essentially connected with the whole universe.

Contemporary humanism still contains some obviously Stoic elements, such as its belief in the solidarity of all peoples based upon their common nature, and in the primacy of reason.

It is perhaps just because Stoicism has never become a full-fledged philosophical system that, many centuries after the dissolution of the Stoic school, fundamental themes of its philosophy have emerged again and again, and many have become incorporated into modern thinking.

Philosophy and natural science

Historical intertwining

The history of philosophy is intertwined with the history of the natural sciences. Long before the 19th century, when the term *science* began to be used with its modern meaning, those who are now counted among the major figures in the history of Western philosophy were often equally famous for their contributions to "natural philosophy," the bundle of inquiries now designated as sciences.

Aristotle (384–322 BCE) was the first great biologist; René Descartes (1596–1650) formulated analytic geometry ("Cartesian geometry") and discovered the laws of the reflection and refraction of light; Gottfried Wilhelm Leibniz (1646–1716) laid claim to priority in the invention of the calculus; and Immanuel Kant (1724–1804) offered the basis of a still-current hypothesis regarding the formation of the solar system (the Kant-Laplace nebular hypothesis).

In reflecting on human knowledge, the great philosophers also offered accounts of the aims and methods of the sciences, ranging from Aristotle's studies in logic through the proposals of Francis Bacon (1561–1626) and Descartes, which were instrumental in shaping 17th-century science.

They were joined in these reflections by the most eminent natural scientists. Galileo (1564–1642) supplemented his arguments about the motions of earthly and heavenly bodies with claims about the roles of mathematics and experiment in discovering facts about nature.

Similarly, the account given by Isaac Newton (1642–1727) of his system of the natural world is punctuated by a defence of

69

his methods and an outline of a positive program for scientific inquiry. Antoine-Laurent Lavoisier (1743–94), James Clerk Maxwell (1831–79), Charles Darwin (1809–82), and Albert Einstein (1879–1955) all continued this tradition, offering their own insights into the character of the scientific enterprise.

Although it may sometimes be difficult to decide whether to classify an older figure as a philosopher or a scientist—and, indeed, the archaic "natural philosopher" may sometimes seem to provide a good compromise—since the early 20th century, philosophy of science has been more self-conscious about its proper role.

Some philosophers continue to work on problems that are continuous with the natural sciences, exploring, for example, the character of space and time or the fundamental features of life.

They contribute to the philosophy of the special sciences, a field with a long tradition of distinguished work in the philosophy of physics and with more-recent contributions in the philosophy of biology and the philosophy of psychology and neuroscience.

General philosophy of science, by contrast, seeks to illuminate broad features of the sciences, continuing the inquiries begun in Aristotle's discussions of logic and method. This is the topic of the present article.

Logical positivism and empiricism

A series of developments in early 20th-century philosophy made the general philosophy of science central to philosophy in the English-speaking world.

Inspired by the articulation of mathematical logic, or formal logic, in the work of the philosophers Gottlob Frege (1848–1925) and Bertrand Russell (1872–1970) and the mathematician David Hilbert (1862–1943), a group of European philosophers known as the Vienna Circle attempted to diagnose the difference between the inconclusive debates that mark the history of philosophy and the firm accomplishments of the sciences they admired.

They offered criteria of meaningfulness, or "cognitive significance," aiming to demonstrate that traditional philosophical questions (and their proposed answers) are meaningless.

The correct task of philosophy, they suggested, is to formulate a "logic of the sciences" that would be analogous to the logic of pure mathematics formulated by Frege, Russell, and Hilbert. In the light of logic, they thought, genuinely fruitful inquiries could be freed from the encumbrances of traditional philosophy.

To carry through this bold program, a sharp criterion of meaningfulness was required. Unfortunately, as they tried to use the tools of mathematical logic to specify the criterion, the logical positivists (as they came to be known) encountered unexpected difficulties.

Again and again, promising proposals were either so lax that they allowed the cloudiest pronouncements of traditional metaphysics to count as meaningful, or so restrictive that they excluded the most cherished hypotheses of the.

71

Faced with these discouraging results, logical positivism evolved into a more moderate movement, logical empiricism. (Many historians of philosophy treat this movement as a late version of logical positivism and accordingly do not refer to it by any distinct name.)

Logical empiricists took as central the task of understanding the distinctive virtues of the natural sciences. In effect, they proposed that the search for a theory of scientific method— undertaken by Aristotle, Bacon, Descartes, and others— could be carried out more thoroughly with the tools of mathematical logic.

They saw a theory of scientific method as central to philosophy and they also viewed that theory as valuable for aspiring areas of inquiry in which an explicit understanding of method might resolve debates and clear away confusions.

Their agenda was deeply influential in subsequent philosophy of science.

Discovery, justification, and falsification

Logics of discovery and justification

An ideal theory of scientific method would consist of instructions that could lead an investigator from ignorance to knowledge.

Descartes and Bacon sometimes wrote as if they could offer so ideal a theory, but after the mid-20th century the orthodox view was that this is too much to ask for. Following Hans Reichenbach (1891–1953), philosophers often distinguished between the "context of discovery" and the "context of justification."

Once a hypothesis has been proposed, there are canons of logic that determine whether or not it should be accepted— that is, there are rules of method that hold in the context of justification.

There are, however, no such rules that will guide someone to formulate the right hypothesis, or even hypotheses that are plausible or fruitful.

The logical empiricists were led to this conclusion by reflecting on cases in which scientific discoveries were made either by imaginative leaps or by lucky accidents; a favourite example was the hypothesis by August Kekulé (1829–96) that benzene molecules have a hexagonal structure, allegedly formed as he was dozing in front of a fire in which the live coals seemed to resemble a snake devouring its own tail.

Although the idea that there cannot be a logic of scientific discovery often assumed the status of orthodoxy, it was not unquestioned.

One of the implications of the influential work of Thomas Kuhn (1922–96) in the philosophy of science was that considerations of the likelihood of future discoveries of particular kinds are sometimes entangled with judgments of evidence.

So discovery can be dismissed as an irrational process only if one is prepared to concede that the irrationality also infects the context of justification itself.

Sometimes in response to Kuhn and sometimes for independent reasons, philosophers tried to analyze particular instances of complex scientific discoveries, showing how the scientists involved appear to have followed identifiable methods and strategies.

The most ambitious response to the empiricist orthodoxy tried to do exactly what was abandoned as hopeless—to wit, specify formal procedures for producing hypotheses in response to an available body of evidence.

So, for example, the American philosopher Clark Glymour and his associates wrote computer programs to generate hypotheses in response to statistical evidence, hypotheses that often introduced new variables that did not themselves figure in the data.

These programs were applied in various traditionally difficult areas of natural and social scientific research. Perhaps, then, logical empiricism was premature in writing off the context of discovery as beyond the range of philosophical analysis.

In contrast, logical empiricists worked vigorously on the problem of understanding scientific justification. Inspired by the thought that Frege, Russell, and Hilbert had given a completely precise specification of the conditions under which premises deductively imply a conclusion, philosophers of science hoped to offer a "logic of confirmation" that would identify, with equal precision, the conditions under which a body of evidence supported a scientific hypothesis.

They recognized, of course, that a series of experimental reports on the expansion of metals under heat would not deductively imply the general conclusion that all metals expand when heated—for even if all the reports were correct, it would still be possible that the very next metal to be examined failed to expand under heat.

Nonetheless, it seemed that a sufficiently large and sufficiently varied collection of reports would provide some support, even strong support, for the generalization. The philosophical task was to make precise this intuitive judgment about support.

Bayesian confirmation

That conclusion was extended in the most prominent contemporary approach to issues of confirmation, so-called Bayesianism, named for the English clergyman and mathematician Thomas Bayes (1702–61). The guiding thought of Bayesianism is that acquiring evidence modifies the probability rationally assigned to a hypothesis.

Any use of Bayes's theorem to reconstruct scientific reasoning plainly depends on the idea that scientists can assign the pertinent probabilities, both the prior probabilities and the probabilities of the evidence conditional on various hypotheses.

But how should scientists conclude that the probability of an interesting hypothesis takes on a particular value or that a

75

certain evidential finding would be extremely improbable if the interesting hypothesis were false?

The simple example about drawing from a deck of cards is potentially misleading in this respect, because in this case there seems to be available a straightforward means of calculating the probability that a specific card, such as the king of hearts, will be drawn.

There is no obvious analogue with respect to scientific hypotheses. It would seem foolish, for example, to suppose that there is some list of potential scientific hypotheses, each of which is equally likely to hold true of the universe.

Bayesians are divided in their responses to this difficulty. A relatively small minority—the so-called "objective" Bayesians—hope to find objective criteria for the rational assignment of prior probabilities.

The majority position—"subjective" Bayesianism, sometimes also called personalism—supposes, by contrast, that no such criteria are to be found. The only limits on rational choice of prior probabilities stem from the need to give each truth of logic and mathematics the probability 1 and to provide a value different from both 0 and 1 for every empirical statement.

The former proviso reflects the view that the laws of logic and mathematics cannot be false; the latter embodies the idea that any statement whose truth or falsity is not determined by the laws of logic and mathematics might turn out to be true (or false).

On the face of it, subjective Bayesianism appears incapable of providing any serious reconstruction of scientific reasoning.

Thus, imagine two scientists of the late 17th century who differ in their initial assessments of Newton's account of the motions of the heavenly bodies.

One begins by assigning the Newtonian hypothesis a small but significant probability; the other attributes a probability that is truly minute.

As they collect evidence, both modify their probability judgments in accordance with Bayes's theorem, and, in both instances, the probability of the Newtonian hypothesis goes up.

For the first scientist it approaches 1. The second, however, has begun with so minute a probability that, even with a large body of positive evidence for the Newtonian hypothesis, the final value assigned is still tiny.

From the subjective Bayesian perspective, both have proceeded impeccably. Yet, at the end of the day, they diverge quite radically in their assessment of the hypothesis.

If one supposes that the evidence obtained is like that acquired in the decades after the publication of Newton's hypothesis in his *Principia* (*Philosophiae naturalis principia mathematica*, 1687), it may seem possible to resolve the issue as follows: even though both investigators were initially sceptical (both assigned small prior probabilities to Newton's hypothesis), one gave the hypothesis a serious chance and the other did not; the inquirer who started with the truly minute probability made an irrational judgment that infects the conclusion.

The Newtonian hypothesis is not a logical or mathematical truth (or a logical or mathematical falsehood), and both scientists give it a probability different from 0 and 1. By subjective Bayesian standards, that is all rational inquirers are asked to do.

The orthodox response to worries of this type is to offer mathematical theorems that demonstrate how individuals starting with different prior probabilities will eventually converge on a common value.

Indeed, were the imaginary investigators to keep going long enough, their eventual assignments of probability would differ by an amount as tiny as one cared to make it. In the long run, scientists who lived by Bayesian standards would agree.

But, as the English economist (and contributor to the theory of probability and confirmation) John Maynard Keynes (1883–1946) once observed, "in the long run we are all dead."

Scientific decisions are inevitably made in a finite period of time, and the same mathematical explorations that yield convergence theorems will also show that, given a fixed period for decision making, however long it may be, there can be people who satisfy the subjective Bayesian requirements and yet remain about as far apart as possible, even at the end of the evidence-gathering period.

Explanations, laws, and theories

The logical-empiricist project of contrasting the virtues of science with the defects of other human ventures was only partly carried out by attempting to understand the logic of scientific justification.

In addition, empiricists hoped to analyze the forms of scientific knowledge. They saw the sciences as arriving at laws of nature that were systematically assembled into theories.

Laws and theories were valuable not only for providing bases for prediction and intervention but also for yielding explanation of natural phenomena.

In some discussions, philosophers also envisaged an ultimate aim for the systematic and explanatory work of the sciences: the construction of a unified science in which nature was understood in maximum depth.

The idea that the aims of the natural sciences are explanation, prediction, and control dates back at least to the 19th century.

Early in the 20th century, however, some prominent scholars of science were inclined to dismiss the ideal of explanation, contending that explanation is inevitably a subjective matter.

Explanation, it was suggested, is a matter of feeling "at home" with the phenomena, and good science need provide nothing of the sort. It is enough if it achieves accurate predictions and an ability to control.

Difficulties

One obvious line of objection is that explanations, in ordinary life as well as in the sciences, rarely take the form of complete arguments.

A clumsy person, for example, may explain why there is a stain on the carpet by confessing that he spilled the coffee, and a geneticist may account for an unusual fruit fly by

79

claiming that there was a recombination of the parental genotypes.

Hempel responded to this criticism by distinguishing between what is actually presented to someone who requests an explanation (the "explanation sketch") and the full objective explanation.

A reply to an explanation seeker works because the explanation sketch can be combined with information that the person already possesses to enable him to arrive at the full explanation.

The explanation sketch gains its explanatory force from the full explanation and contains the part of the full explanation that the questioner needs to know.

A second difficulty for Hempel's account resulted from his candid admission that he was unable to offer a full analysis of the notion of a scientific law.

Laws are generalisations about a range of natural phenomena, sometimes universal ("Any two bodies attract one another with a force that is proportional to the product of their masses and inversely as the square of the distance between them") and sometimes statistical ("The chance that any particular allele will be transmitted to a gamete in meiosis is 50 percent"). Not every generalization, however, counts as a scientific law.

There are streets on which every house is made of brick, but no judgment of the form "All houses on X street are made of brick" qualifies as a scientific law. As Reichenbach pointed out, there are accidental generalizations that seem to have very broad scope.

Whereas the statement "All uranium spheres have a radius of less than one kilometre" is a matter of natural law (large uranium spheres would be unstable because of fundamental physical properties), the statement "All gold spheres have a radius of less than one kilometre" merely expresses a cosmic accident.

Intuitively, laws of nature seem to embody a kind of necessity: they do not simply describe the way that things happen to be, but, in some sense, they describe how things have to be. If one attempted to build a very large uranium sphere, one would be bound to fail.

The prevalent attitude of logical empiricism, following the celebrated discussion of "necessary connections" in nature by the Scottish philosopher David Hume (1711–76), was to be wary of invoking notions of necessity.

To be sure, logical empiricists recognized the necessity of logic and mathematics, but the laws of nature could hardly be conceived as necessary in this sense, for it is logically (and mathematically) possible that the universe had different laws.

Indeed, one main hope of Hempel and his colleagues was to avoid difficulties with necessity by relying on the concepts of law and explanation. To say that there is a necessary connection between two types of events is, they proposed, simply to assert a law-like succession—events of the first type are regularly succeeded by events of the second, and the succession is a matter of natural law.

For this program to succeed, however, logical empiricism required an analysis of the notion of a law of nature that did not rely on the concept of necessity.

Logical empiricists were admirably clear about what they wanted and about what had to be done to achieve it, but the project of providing the pertinent analysis of laws of nature remained an open problem for them.

Scruples about necessary connections also generated a third class of difficulties for Hempel's project. There are examples of arguments that fit the patterns approved by Hempel and yet fail to count as explanatory, at least by ordinary lights. Imagine a flagpole that casts a shadow on the ground.

One can explain the length of the shadow by deducing it (using trigonometry) from the height of the pole, the angle of elevation of the Sun, and the law of light propagation (i.e., the law that light travels in straight lines). So far this is unproblematic, for the little argument just outlined accords with Hempel's model of explanation.

Notice, however, that there is a simple way to switch one of the premises with the conclusion: if one starts with the length of the shadow, the angle of elevation of the Sun, and the law of light propagation, one can deduce (using trigonometry) the height of the pole. The new derivation also accords with Hempel's model.

But this is perturbing, because, while one thinks of the height of a pole as explaining the length of a shadow, one does not think of the length of a shadow as explaining the height of a pole.

Intuitively, the amended derivation gets things backward, reversing the proper order of dependence. Given the commitments of logical empiricism, however, these diagnoses make no sense, and the two arguments are on a par with respect to explanatory power.

Although Hempel was sometimes inclined to "bite the bullet" and defend the explanatory worth of both arguments, most philosophers concluded that something was lacking.

Furthermore, it seemed obvious what the missing ingredient was: shadows are causally dependent on poles in a way in which poles are not causally dependent on shadows. Since explanation must respect dependencies, the amended derivation is explanatorily worthless.

Like the concept of natural necessity, however, the notion of causal dependence was anathema to logical empiricists— both had been targets of Hume's famous critique. To develop a satisfactory account of explanatory asymmetry, therefore, the logical empiricists needed to capture the idea of causal dependence by formulating conditions on genuine explanation in an acceptable idiom. Here too Hempel's program proved unsuccessful.

The fourth and last area in which trouble surfaced was in the treatment of probabilistic explanation. As discussed in the preceding section (Discovery, justification, and falsification), the probability ascribed to an outcome may vary, even quite dramatically, when new information is added.

Hempel appreciated the point, recognizing that some statistical arguments that satisfy his conditions on explanation have the property that, even though all the premises are true, the support they lend to the conclusion would be radically undermined by adding extra premises.

He attempted to solve the problem by adding further requirements. It was shown, however, that the new conditions were either ineffective or else trivialized the activity of probabilistic explanation.

Nor is it obvious that the fundamental idea of explaining through making the phenomena expectable can be sustained.

To cite a famous example, one can explain the fact that the mayor contracted paresis by pointing out that he had previously had untreated syphilis; even though only 8 to 10 percent of people with untreated syphilis go on to develop paresis.

In this instance, there is no statistical argument that confers high probability on the conclusion that the mayor contracted paresis—that conclusion remains improbable in light of the information advanced (85 percent of those with untreated syphilis do not get paresis).

What seems crucial is the increase in probability, the fact that the probability of the conclusion rose from truly minute (paresis is extremely rare in the general population) to significant.

Scientific laws

Similar uncertainties affect recent discussions of scientific laws. As already noted, logical empiricism faced a difficult problem in distinguishing between genuine laws and accidental generalizations.

Just as theorists of explanation sometimes liberated themselves from hard problems by invoking a concept hitherto held as taboo—the notion of causation—so too some philosophers championed an idea of natural necessity and tried to characterize it as precisely as possible.

Others, more sympathetic to Hume's suspicions, continued the logical-empiricist project of analyzing the notion independently of the concept of natural necessity.

The most important approach along these lines identifies the laws of nature as the generalizations that would figure in the best systematization of all natural phenomena.

This suggestion fits naturally with the unificationist approach to explanation but encounters similar difficulties in articulating the idea of a "best systematization." Perhaps more fundamentally, it is not obvious that the concept of "all natural phenomena" is coherent (or, even if it is, whether this is something in which science should be interested).

There is an even more basic issue. Why is the notion of a scientific law of any philosophical interest? Within the framework of logical empiricism, and specifically within Hempel's approach to explanation, there was a clear answer.

Explanations depend on laws, and the notion of law is to be explicated without appeal to suspect notions such as natural necessity. But Hempel's approach is now defunct, and many contemporary philosophers are suspicious of the old suspicions, prepared to be more tolerant of appeals to causation and natural necessity. What function, then, would an account of laws now serve?

Perhaps the thought is that the search for the laws of nature is central to the scientific enterprise. But, to begin with, the scientific habit of labelling certain statements as "laws" seems extremely haphazard.

There are areas, moreover, in which it is hard to find any laws—large tracts of the life and earth sciences, for example—and yet scientists in these areas are credited with the most important discoveries. James Watson and Francis Crick (1916–2004) won a Nobel Prize for one of the greatest scientific achievements of the 20th century (indeed, arguably the most fruitful), but it would be hard to state the law that they discovered.

Accordingly, philosophers of science are beginning to abandon the notion that laws are central to science, focusing instead on the search for symmetries in physics, on the differing uses of approximate generalizations in biology, and on the deployment of models in numerous areas of the sciences.

Axiomatic conception

In similar fashion, contemporary philosophy of science is moving beyond the question of the structure of scientific theories. For a variety of reasons, that question was of enormous importance to the logical positivists and to the logical empiricists.

Mathematical logic supplied a clear conception: a theory is a collection of statements (the axioms of the theory) and their deductive consequences.

The logical positivists showed how this conception could be applied in scientific cases—one could axiomatise the theory of relativity, for example. Nor was the work of axiomatisation an idle exercise, for the difficulties of formulating a precise criterion of cognitive significance (intended to separate good science from meaningless philosophical discussion) raised questions about the legitimacy of the special vocabulary that figures in scientific theories.

Convinced that the sound and fury of German metaphysics—references to "Absolute Spirit" by Georg Wilhelm Friedrich Hegel (1770–1831) and talk of "the Nothing" by Martin Heidegger (1889–1976)—signified, indeed, nothing, logical positivists (and logical empiricists) recognized that they needed to show how terms such as *electron* and *covalent bond* were different.

They began from a distinction between two types of language. Observational language comprises all the terms that can be acquired by presentation of observable samples.

Although they were sceptical about mixing psychology and philosophy, logical empiricists tacitly adopted a simple theory of learning: children can learn terms such as *red* by being shown appropriate swatches, *hot* by holding their hands under the right taps, and so forth.

Logical empiricists denied that this observational vocabulary would suffice to define the special terms of theoretical science, the theoretical language that seemed to pick out unobservable entities and properties.

Conceiving of theories as axiomatic systems, however, they drew a distinction between two types of axioms. Some axioms contain only theoretical vocabulary, while others contain both theoretical and observational terms.

The latter, variously characterized as "correspondence rules" or "coordinating definitions," relate the theoretical and observational vocabularies, and it is through them that theoretical terms acquire what meaning they have. The last formulation blurs an important difference between two schools within logical empiricism.

According to one school, the theoretical terms are "partially interpreted" by the correspondence rules, so, for example, if one such rule is that an electron produces a particular kind of track in a cloud chamber, then many possibilities for the meaning of the previously unfamiliar term *electron* are ruled out.

87

A more radical school, instrumentalism, held that, strictly speaking, the theoretical vocabulary remains meaningless. Instrumentalists took scientific theories to be axiomatic systems only part of whose vocabulary—the observational language—is interpreted; the rest is a formal calculus whose purpose is to yield predictions couched in the observational vocabulary.

Even instrumentalists, however, were able to maintain a distinction between serious theoretical science and the much-derided metaphysics, for their reconstructions of scientific theories would reveal the uninterpreted vocabulary as playing an important functional role (a result not to be expected in the metaphysical case).

Logical empiricists debated the merits of the two stances, exploring the difficulties of making precise the notion of partial interpretation and the possibility of finding axiomatic systems that would generate all the observational consequences without employing any theoretical vocabulary.

Their exchanges were effectively undercut by the American philosopher Hilary Putnam, who recognized that the initial motivation for the approach to theories was deeply problematic. In their brief sketches of the differences between the two languages, logical empiricists had conflated two distinctions.

On the one hand there is a contrast between things that can be observed and things that cannot—the observable-unobservable distinction; on the other hand, there is the difference between terms whose meanings can be acquired through demonstration and those whose meanings cannot be acquired in this way—the observational-theoretical distinction.

It is a mistake to believe that the distinctions are congruent, that observational terms apply to observable things and theoretical terms to unobservable things. In the first place, many theoretical terms apply to observables (*spectroscope* is an example).

More important, many terms learnable through demonstration apply to un-observables—in Putnam's telling example, even small children learn to talk of "people too little to see."

Once the second point was appreciated, the way was open for introducing theoretical vocabulary that logical empiricism had never taken seriously (even though many eminent scientists and gifted science teachers had often developed such modes of conveying meaning).

One can see that the term *part* might be learned in connection with pieces of observable objects and that its use might cover unobservable things as well, so the specification of atoms as "parts of all matter that themselves have no parts" (whatever its merits today) might have served the contemporaries of John Dalton (1766–1844), an early developer of atomic theory, as a means of appreciating what he was claiming.

Logical empiricism lavished great attention on the problem of exposing the structure of scientific theories because solving that problem seemed crucial to the vindication of the theoretical vocabulary employed by the sciences. Putnam showed, in effect, that no such strenuous efforts were required.

Semantic conception

Starting in the 1960s, philosophers of science explored alternative approaches to scientific theories.

Prominent among them was the so-called semantic conception, originally formulated by Patrick Suppes, according to which theories are viewed as collections of models together with hypotheses about how these models relate to parts of nature.

Versions of the semantic conception differ in their views about the character of models, sometimes taking models to be abstract mathematical structures, susceptible to precise formal specifications, and sometimes taking them to be more concrete (as chemists do, for example, when they build models of particular molecules).

The semantic conception of theories has several attractive features.

- First, unlike the older approach, it provides a way of discussing aspects of science that are independent of the choice of a particular language.

- Second, it appears to do far more justice to areas of science in which theoretical achievements resist axiomatisation.

Darwinian evolutionary theory is a case in point. During the heyday of the axiomatic approach, a few philosophers attempted to show how the theory of evolution could be brought within the orthodox conception of theories, but their efforts tended to produce formal theories that bordered on triviality.

The consequent debates about whether the theory of evolution was more than a tautology should have generated serious philosophical embarrassment. Philosophers deploying the semantic conception, by contrast, shed light on theoretical issues that arise in contemporary evolutionary biology.

Finally, the semantic conception is far better suited to an aspect of the sciences that was frequently neglected, the practice of idealization.

Instead of thinking of scientists as aspiring to offer literally correct descriptions of general features of the world, the semantic conception supposes that they propose models accompanied by claims that particular parts of nature correspond to these models in specific respects and to specific degrees.

Unification and reduction

One large question about scientific theories that excites philosophical and scientific attention concerns the possibility of producing a single theory that will encompass the domains of all the sciences.

Many thinkers are attracted by the idea of a unified science, or by the view that the sciences form a hierarchy. There is a powerful intuitive argument for this attitude.

If one considers the subject matter of the social sciences, for example, it seems that social phenomena are the product of people standing in complicated relations to each other and acting in complicated ways.

These people, of course, are complex biological and psychological systems. Their psychological activity is grounded in the neural firings in their brains. Hence, people are intricate biological systems.

91

The intricacies of biology are based on the choreography of molecular reactions within and between individual cells. Biology, then, is very complicated chemistry.

Chemical reactions themselves involve the forming and breaking of bonds, and these are matters of microphysics.

At the end of the day, therefore, all natural phenomena, even those involving interactions between people, are no more than an exceptionally complicated series of transactions between the ultimate physical constituents of matter.

A complete account of those ultimate constituents and their interactions would thus amount to a "theory of everything."

Political philosophy

Political opinion

Politics and its philosophical interpretation is branch of philosophy that is concerned, at the most abstract level, with the concepts and arguments involved in political opinion.

The meaning of the term *political* is itself one of the major problems of political philosophy. Broadly, however, one may characterize as political all those practices and institutions that are concerned with government.

The central problem of political philosophy is how to deploy or limit public power so as to maintain the survival and enhance the quality of human life.

Like all aspects of human experience, political philosophy is conditioned by environment and by the scope and limitations of mind, and the answers given by successive political philosophers to perennial problems reflect the knowledge and the assumptions of their times.

Political philosophy, as distinct from the study of political and administrative organization, is more theoretical and normative than descriptive.

It is inevitably related to general philosophy and is itself a subject of cultural anthropology, sociology, and the sociology of knowledge.

As a normative discipline it is thus concerned with what ought, on various assumptions, to be and how this purpose can be promoted, rather than with a description of facts—

93

although any realistic political theory is necessarily related to these facts.

The political philosopher is thus not concerned so much, for example, with how pressure groups work or how, by various systems of voting, decisions are arrived at as with what the aims of the whole political process should be in the light of a particular philosophy of life.

There is thus a distinction between political philosophy, which reflects the world outlook of successive theorists and which demands an appreciation of their historical settings, and modern political science proper, which, insofar as it can be called a science, is empirical and descriptive.

Political philosophy, however, is not merely unpractical speculation, though it may give rise to highly impractical myths: it is a vitally important aspect of life, and one that, for good or evil, has had decisive results on political action, for the assumptions on which political life is conducted clearly must influence what actually happens.

Political philosophy may thus be viewed as one of the most important intellectual disciplines, for it sets standards of judgment and defines constructive purposes for the use of public power.

Such consideration of the purposes for which power should be used is in a sense more urgent today than it was in earlier periods, for humankind has at its disposal the power either to create a world civilization in which modern technology can benefit the human race or to destroy itself in pursuit of political myths.

The scope for political philosophy is thus great, the clarification of its purpose and limitations urgent—an aspect, indeed, of civilization's survival.

Despite this unique aspect of the contemporary situation, and although ancient political philosophies were formulated under very different conditions, their study still illuminates vital questions today.

Questions concerning the aims of government, the grounds of political obligation, the rights of individuals against the state, the basis of sovereignty, the relation of executive to legislative power, and the nature of political liberty and social justice have been asked and answered in many ways over the centuries.

They are all fundamental to political philosophy and demand answers in terms of modern knowledge and opinion.

International law

According to Bentham's classic definition, international law is a collection of rules governing relations between states. It is a mark of how far international law has evolved that this original definition omits individuals and international organizations—two of the most dynamic and vital elements of modern international law.

Furthermore, it is no longer accurate to view international law as simply a collection of rules; rather, it is a rapidly developing complex of rules and influential—though not directly binding—principles, practices, and assertions coupled with increasingly sophisticated structures and processes.

In its broadest sense, international law provides normative guidelines as well as methods, mechanisms, and a common conceptual language to international actors—i.e., primarily sovereign states but also increasingly international organizations and some individuals.

The range of subjects and actors directly concerned with international law has widened considerably, moving beyond the classical questions of war, peace, and diplomacy to include human rights, economic and trade issues, space law, and international organizations.

Although international law is a legal order and not an ethical one, it has been influenced significantly by ethical principles and concerns, particularly in the sphere of human rights.

Knowledge; Reason and Harmony

Followers of Stoicism offer for consideration various metaphysical systems, united chiefly by their ethical implications.

All variants on the pantheistic theme that the world constitutes a single, organically unified and benevolent whole, in which apparent evil results only from our limited view. Their philosophy had at its core the beliefs that virtue is based on: Knowledge; Reason and Harmony.

The changes of circumstances were viewed with evenness of mind: pleasure, pain, and even death were irrelevant to true happiness. In time, the idea that only the accomplished wise man (the philosopher) could attain virtue was challenged, and Stoicism became more relevant to the reality of politics and statesmen.

The Stoic belief in the brotherhood of man helped philosophy to make a real impact in later Republican Rome; upon such men as the young Cato (whose suicide brought him a martyr's fame), Brutus, and Cicero.

Later it underlay much aristocratic opposition to the emperors, but even so its disciples included Seneca, tutor and adviser to Nero and the emperor Marcus Aurelius.

END

Index   Page

Andreas Sofroniou

Bibliography

ALL BOOKS LISTED BELOW ARE PUBLISHED BY ANDREAS SOFRONIOU

1. THERAPEUTIC PSYCHOLOGY, ISBN: 978-1-326-34523-5
2. MEDICAL ETHICS THROUGH THE AGES, ISBN: 978-1-4092- 7468-1
3. MEDICAL ETHICS, FROM HIPPOCRATES TO THE 21ST CENTURY ISBN: 978-1-4457-1203-1
4. MISINTERPRETATION OF SIGMUND FREUD, ISBN: 978-1-4467-1659-5
5. JUNG'S PSYCHOTHERAPY: THE PSYCHOLOGICAL & MYTHOLOGICAL METHODS, ISBN: 978-1-4477-4740-6
6. FREUDIAN ANALYSIS & JUNGIAN SYNTHESIS, ISBN: 978-1-4477-5996-6
7. ADLER'S INDIVIDUAL PSYCHOLOGY AND RELATED METHODS, ISBN: 978-1-291-85951-5
8. ADLERIAN INDIVIDUALISM , JUNGIAN SYNTHESIS, FREUDIAN ANALYSIS, ISBN: 978-1-291-85937-9
9. PSYCHOTHERAPY, CONCEPTS OF TREATMENT, ISBN: 978-1-291-50178-0
10. PSYCHOLOGY, CONCEPTS OF BEHAVIOUR, ISBN: 978-1-291-47573-9
11. PHILOSOPHY FOR HUMAN BEHAVIOUR, ISBN: 978-1-291-12707-2
12. SEX, AN EXPLORATION OF SEXUALITY, EROS AND LOVE, ISBN: 978-1-291-56931-5
13. PSYCHOLOGY FROM CONCEPTION TO SENILITY, ISBN: 978-1-4092-7218-2
14. PSYCHOLOGY OF CHILD CULTURE, ISBN: 978-1-4092-7619-7
15. JOYFUL PARENTING, ISBN: 0 9527956 1 2
16. GUIDE TO A JOYFUL PARENTING, ISBN: 0 952 7956 1 2
17. THERAPEUTIC PHILOSOPHY FOR THE INDIVIDUAL AND THE STATE, ISBN: 978-1-4092-7586-2
18. PHILOSOPHIC COUNSELLING FOR PEOPLE AND THEIR GOVERNMENTS, ISBN: 978-1-4092-7400-1
19. CHILD PSYCHOTHERAPY, ISBN: 978-1-326-44169-2
20. HYPNOTHERAPY IN MEDICINE, PSYCHOLOGY, MAGIC, ISBN: 978-1-326-48163-6
21. ART FOR PSYCHOTHERAPY, ISBN: 978-1-326-78959-6
22. SLEEPING AND DREAMING EXPLAINED BY ARTS & SCIENCE, ISBN: ISBN: 978-1-326-81309-3
23. PHILOSOPHY AND POLITICS, ISBN: 978-1-326-33854-1
24. MORAL PHILOSOPHY, FROM SOCRATES TO THE 21ST AEON, ISBN: 978-1-4457-4618-0
25. MORAL PHILOSOPHY, FROM HIPPOCRATES TO THE 21ST AEON, ISBN: 978-1-84753-463-7
26. MORAL PHILOSOPHY, THE ETHICAL APPROACH THROUGH THE AGES, ISBN: 978-1-4092-7703-3
27. MORAL PHILOSOPHY, ISBN: 978-1-4478-5037-3
28. 2011 POLITICS, ORGANISATIONS, PSYCHOANALYSIS, POETRY, ISBN: 978-1-4467-2741-6
29. WISDOM AN ACCUMULATION OF KNOWLEDGE, ISBN: 978-1-326-99692-5
30. MYTHOLOGY LEGENDS FROM AROUND THE GLOBE, ISBN: 978-1-326-98630-8
31. PLATO'S EPISTEMOLOGY, ISBN: 978-1-4716-6584-4
32. ARISTOTLE'S AETIOLOGY, ISBN: 978-1-4716-7861-5
33. MARXISM, SOCIALISM & COMMUNISM, ISBN: 978-1-4716-8236-0
34. MACHIAVELLI'S POLITICS & RELEVANT PHILOSOPHICAL CONCEPTS, ISBN: 978-1-4716-8629-0
35. BRITISH PHILOSOPHERS, 16TH TO 18TH CENTURY, ISBN: 978-1-4717-1072-8
36. ROUSSEAU ON WILL AND MORALITY, ISBN: 978-1-4717-1070-4
37. EPISTEMOLOGY, A SYSTEMATIC OVERVIEW, ISBN: 978-1-326-11380-3
38. HEGEL ON IDEALISM, KNOWLEDGE & REALITY, ISBN: 978-1-4717-0954-8
39. METAPHYSICS FACTS AND FALLACIES, ISBN: 978-1-326-80745-0
40. SOCIAL SCIENCES AND PHILOLOGY, ISBN: 978-1-326-33840-4
41. PHILOLOGY, CONCEPTS OF EUROPEAN LITERATURE, ISBN: 978-1-291-49148-7
42. THREE MILLENNIA OF HELLENIC PHILOLOGY, ISBN: 978-1-291-49799-1
43. CYPRUS, PERMANENT DEPRIVATION OF FREEDOM, ISBN: 978-1-291-50833-8
44. SOCIOLOGY, CONCEPTS OF GROUP BEHAVIOUR, ISBN: 978-1-291-51888-7
45. SOCIAL SCIENCES, CONCEPTS OF BRANCHES AND RELATIONSHIPS ISBN: 978-1-291-52321-8

46. CONCEPTS OF SOCIAL SCIENTISTS AND GREAT THINKERS, ISBN: 978-1-291-53786-4
47. EMPIRES AND COLONIALISM ISBN: 978-1-326-46761-6
48. CYPRUS, COLONISED BY MOST EMPIRES, ISBN, 978-1-326-47164-4
49. PERICLES, GOLDEN AGE OF ATHENS, ISBN: 978-1-326-47592-5
50. TRIANGLE OF EDUCATION TRAINING EXPERIENCE, ISBN: 978-1- 326-82934-6
51. HARMONY IS LOVE FRIENDSHIP SEX, ISBN: 978-1-326-85687-8
52. INTERNATIONAL HUMAN RIGHTS, ISBN: 978-1-326-87348-6
53. ANALYSIS OF LOGIC AND SANITY, ISBN: ISBN: 978-1-326-90604-7
54. INTERNATIONAL LAW, GLOBAL RELATIONS, WORLD POWERS; 978-1-326-92921-3
55. MANAGEMENT SCIENCE AND BUSINESS, ISBN: 978-1-326-45508-8
56. ECONOMICS WORLD HOUSE RULES, ISBN: 978-1-326-96162-6
57. POLITICAL SYSTEMS NORMS AND LAWS, ISBN: 978-1-326-97404-6
58. HISTORY OF SYSTEMS, ENGINEERING, TECHNOLOGY, ISBN: 978-1-326-94420-9
59. INFORMATION TECHNOLOGY AND MANAGEMENT, ISBN: 978-1-326-34496-2
60. I.T. RISK MANAGEMENT, ISBN: 978-1-4467-5653-9
61. SYSTEMS ENGINEERING, ISBN: 978-1-4477-7553-9
62. BUSINESS INFORMATION SYSTEMS, CONCEPTS AND EXAMPLES, ISBN: 978-1-4092-7338-7
63. A GUIDE TO INFORMATION TECHNOLOGY, ISBN: 978-1-4092-7608-1
64. CHANGE MANAGEMENT IN I.T., ISBN: 978-1-4092-7712-5
65. FRONT-END DESIGN AND DEVELOPMENT FOR SYSTEMS APPLICATIONS, ISBN: 978-1-4092-7588-6
66. I.T RISK MANAGEMENT, ISBN: 978-1-4092-7488-9
67. I.T. RISK MANAGEMENT – 2011 EDITION, ISBN: 978-1-4467- 5653-9
68. SIMPLIFIED PROCEDURES FOR I.T. PROJECTS DEVELOPMENT; 978-1-4092-7562-6
69. SIGMA METHODOLOGY FOR RISK MANAGEMENT IN SYSTEMS DEVELOPMENT, ISBN: 978-1-4092-7690-6
70. TRADING ON THE INTERNET IN THE YEAR 2000 AND BEYOND, ISBN: 978-1-4092- 7577
71. STRUCTURED SYSTEMS METHODOLOGY, ISBN: 978-1-4477-6610-0
72. INFORMATION TECHNOLOGY LOGICAL ANALYSIS, ISBN: 978-1-4717-1688-1
73. I.T. RISKS LOGICAL ANALYSIS, ISBN: 978-1-4717-1957-8
74. LOGICAL ANALYSIS OF I.T. CHANGES, ISBN: 978-1-4717-2288-2
75. LOGICAL ANALYSIS OF SYSTEMS, RISKS , CHANGES, ISBN: 978-1-4717-2294-3
76. COMPUTING, A PRÉCIS ON SYSTEMS, SOFTWARE AND HARDWARE, ISBN: 978-1-2910-5102-5
77. MANAGE THAT I.T. PROJECT, ISBN: 978-1-4717-5304-6
78. CHANGE MANAGEMENT, ISBN: 978-1-4457-6114-5
79. MANAGEMENT OF COMMERCIAL COMPUTING, ISBN: 978-1-4092-7550-3
80. PROGRAMME MANAGEMENT WORKSHOP, ISBN: 978-1-4092-7583-1
81. MANAGEMENT OF I.T. CHANGES, RISKS, WORKSHOPS, EPISTEMOLOGY, ISBN: 978-1-84753-147-6
82. THE PHILOSOPHICAL CONCEPTS OF MANAGEMENT THROUGH THE AGES, ISBN: 978-1-4092- 7554-1
83. MANAGEMENT OF PROJECTS, SYSTEMS, INTERNET, AND RISKS, ISBN: 978-1-4092- 7464-3
84. HOW TO CONSTRUCT YOUR RESUMÉ, ISBN: 978-1-4092-7383-7
85. DEFINE THAT SYSTEM, ISBN: 978-1-291-15094-0
86. INFORMATION TECHNOLOGY WORKSHOP, ISBN: 978-1-291-16440-4
87. CHANGE MANAGEMENT IN SYSTEMS, ISBN: 978-1-4457-1099-0
88. SYSTEMS MANAGEMENT, ISBN: 978-1-4710-4907-1
89. TECHNOLOGY, A STUDY OF MECHANICAL ARTS AND APPLIED SCIENCES, ISBN: 978-1-291-58550-6
90. EXPERT SYSTEMS, KNOWLEDGE ENGINEERING FOR HUMAN REPLICATION, ISBN: 978-1-291- 59509-3
91. ARTIFICIAL INTELLIGENCE AND INFORMATION TECHNOLOGY, ISBN: 978-1-291- 60445-0
92. PROJECT MANAGEMENT PROCEDURES FOR SYSTEMS DEVELOPMENT, ISBN: 978-0-952-72531-2
93. SURFING THE INTERNET, THEN, NOW, LATER. ISBN: 978-1–291-77653-9
94. ANALYTICAL DIAGRAMS FOR I.T. SYSTEMS, ISBN: 978-1-326-05786-2
95. INTEGRATION OF INFORMATION TECHNOLOGY, ISBN: 978-1-312-64303-1
96. TRAINING FOR CHANGES IN I.T. ISBN: 978-1-326-14325-1

www.ingramcontent.com/pod-product-compliance
Lightning Source LLC
Chambersburg PA
CBHW052057270326
41931CB00012B/2794